BFI Film Classics

The BFI Film Classics is a series of books that introduces, interprets and celebrates landmarks of world cinema. Each volume offers an argument for the film's 'classic' status, together with discussion of its production and reception history, its place within a genre or national cinema, an account of its technical and aesthetic importance, and in many cases, the author's personal response to the film.

For a full list of titles available in the series, please visit our website: www.palgrave.com/bfi

'Magnificently concentrated examples of flowing freeform critical poetry.'
Uncut

'A formidable body of work collectively generating some fascinating insights into the evolution of cinema.'
Times Higher Education Supplement

'The series is a landmark in film criticism.'
Quarterly Review of Film and Video

'Possibly the most bountiful book series in the history of film criticism.'
Jonathan Rosenbaum, *Film Comment*

When Harry Met Sally...

Tamar Jeffers McDonald

A BFI book published by Palgrave

First published in 2015 by
PALGRAVE

on behalf of the

BRITISH FILM INSTITUTE
21 Stephen Street, London W1T 1LN
www.bfi.org.uk

There's more to discover about film and television through the BFI. Our world-renowned archive, cinemas, festivals, films, publications and learning resources are here to inspire you.

Palgrave in the UK is an imprint of Macmillan Publishers Limited, registered in England, company number 785998, of 4 Crinan Street, London N1 9XW. Palgrave Macmillan in the US is a division of St Martin's Press LLC, 175 Fifth Avenue, New York, NY 10010. Palgrave is a global imprint of the above companies and is represented throughout the world. Palgrave® and Macmillan® are registered trademarks in the United States, the United Kingdom, Europe and other countries.

Front cover design: Ma+Chr
Series text design: ketchup/SE14
Images from *When Harry Met Sally…* (Rob Reiner, 1989), Castle Rock Entertainment/Nelson Entertainment International; *Working Girl* (Mike Nichols, 1988), Twentieth Century Fox Film Corporation; *Zelig* (Woody Allen, 1983), © Orion Pictures Corporation; *Mr. & Mrs. Smith* (Doug Liman, 2005), © Regency Entertainment, Inc./Monarchy Enterprises S.a.r.l.; *Indiscreet* (Stanley Donen, 1958), © Grandon Productions Ltd; *Pillow Talk* (Michael Gordon, 1959), © Arwin Productions; *Annie Hall* (Woody Allen, 1977), © United Artists Corporation; *Muppets Tonight*, Series 1 Episode 3 (Gary Halvorson, 1996), Jim Henson Productions; *The Ugly Truth* (Robert Luketic, 2009), © Columbia Pictures Industries, Inc/Beverly Blvd LLC; *Kramer vs. Kramer* (Robert Benton, 1979), Stanley Jaffe Productions/Columbia Pictures Corporation; *Friends with Benefits* (Will Gluck, 2011), © Screen Gems, Inc.; *The Graduate* (Mike Nichols, 1967), Embassy Pictures Corporation/Lawrence Turman, Inc.; *Manhattan* (Woody Allen, 1979), © United Artists; *Sleeper* (Woody Allen, 1973), Metro-Goldwyn-Mayer; *What If* (Michael Dowse, 2013), © F Word Productions, Inc./PCF F-Word The Movie, Inc./Kelcom Limited/Fastnet Films.

Set by Cambrian Typesetters, Camberley, Surrey
Printed in China

This book is printed on paper suitable for recycling and made from fully managed and sustained forest sources. Logging, pulping and manufacturing processes are expected to conform to the environmental regulations of the country of origin.

British Library Cataloguing-in-Publication Data
A catalogue record for this book is available from the British Library
A catalog record for this book is available from the Library of Congress

ISBN 978-1-84457-907-5

Contents

Introduction and Acknowledgments

New York magazine's popular culture blog 'Vulture' marked Nora Ephron's death in 2012 with a slideshow dedicated to some of her finest moments, asserting '*When Harry Met Sally* is arguably the greatest romcom of all time.'[1] The site stayed true to its love for the film in 2014 when it celebrated its twenty-fifth anniversary with a week's worth of articles, again concluding that it had "revolutionized" the romantic comedy genre.[2]

Although the film does now seem to garner a generally positive response – unlike the reception on its 1989 release – I think it still remains a misunderstood film; if it is the favourite of many, it is a relatively unexplored favourite. But it is vital to understand just why *When Harry Met Sally...* is so ground-breaking, as well as warm, funny and poignant, how it departed from both other contemporaneous films and its romcom predecessors, to establish themes and recurrent film elements – tropes – still being employed. Since today's media seem to have united to declare the romantic comedy dead,[3] it is important to identify what made *When Harry Met Sally...* a classic of its kind, in the hope this can lead us to demand and make better films and resuscitate the genre.

Close analysis reveals the film to be carefully and cleverly organised. Along with Nora Ephron's witty script, adroit direction from Rob Reiner, and performances from principals Billy Crystal and Meg Ryan that are both comic and touching, the film's structure plays a significant part in its appeal: while it seems to chart in a loose, organic way the haphazard development of the protagonists' relationship, it takes place within a rigorous framework, enabling a subtle deployment of echoes and parallels across the narrative.

The structure of *When Harry Met Sally...* breaks down into fourteen sections, bracketed by beginning and end credits, and punctuated by seven sequences presenting a married woman and man relating the story of their meeting: the couch couple interludes. I have tried to organise this appreciation and investigation of the film in a similar way, alternating shorter and longer sections; my version of the interludes, like the film's, presents material that may appear tangential but actually casts sidelights on the main story. The longer sections, my equivalent of the movie's narrative segments, examine the bigger thematic elements employed in and across the text.

Before embarking on this exploration, however, a further investigation of the construction is enlightening, revealing not only the skill this entailed, but also the extent to which the structure impacts on the viewer's engagement with and enjoyment of the film.

So although the account of Harry and Sally's relationship seems casual, it is actually laid out in a very schematic way:

Credits
  Couch couple 1
    Narrative segment 1: car ride
  Couch couple 2
    Narrative segment 2: plane ride
  Couch couple 3
    Narrative segment 3: break-ups; new friendship
  Couch couple 4
    Narrative segment 4: friendship, grieving, dating
  Couch couple 5
    Narrative segment 5: dinner for four
  Couch couple 6
    Narrative segment 6: dating, grieving, sex, aftermath
    Narrative segment 7: seasons, grieving, epiphany
  Couch couple 7
Credits

While there is a neat balance in the alternating of couch couple and narrative segments (for all but the last sequence of the film), there are also incidents across and within the narrative segments that chime and echo each other; thus, Sally interrupts Harry kissing his girlfriend in the first section, while he interrupts her kissing her boyfriend in the second, and both interruptions lead to their conversation and antagonism during a period of travel. Both Sally and Harry tell their best friends about their relationship failures in segment 3, and in segment 6, about the failure of their relationship with each other, and so on.

The film's careful structure abounds with echoes, as with these moments of interrupted kisses

The pleasing symmetry established by these parallels and by the recurrence of the chorus-like testimonial sequences from the married couple is disrupted, however, around the one-hour mark. Up until this point, narrative segments of between eleven and sixteen minutes have been bookended by these short couch interludes. After the sixth couple's story, however, the momentum within the narrative picks up, and the recognisable pattern of scenes/testimonial/scenes/testimonial is broken. There is now no break from the main narrative action for thirty-seven minutes until we have the final marital testimonial: Sally and Harry's own.

As will be explored below, the couch couple device is used to forecast and comment on events and emotions in the main narrative; removing this device takes away its Greek chorus effect and adds propulsion to the story, as it moves with inevitability to bringing the protagonists together. In addition, the break from the regular pattern creates an imbalance that we sense; desire for the restitution of the pattern then aligns with a wish for the generically mandated happy ending, making our pleasure even stronger when both are achieved. When we see the final couple talking about their relationship, therefore, satisfaction in seeing them achieve their union is strengthened by enjoyment at this overdue return to the testimonial device.

In the ensuing sections, I will be paying special attention to the film's construction, its innovative handling of traditional romcom tropes and its trailblazing deployment of new ones. It has been a pleasure to explore the film in depth and for this opportunity I must thank Jenna Steventon at Palgrave. In addition, sincere thanks go to Sophia Contento at BFI Publishing, and staff at the Margaret Herrick Library, especially Kristine Kruger. My gratitude and thanks are also due to everyone who helped with sources or texts, and everyone in my support network, including Ann-Marie, Candy, Chloe, Frances, Jessica, Katerina, Lies, Rian, Rosa, Sarah and, of course, Paul, who demonstrates to me every day that men and women can be best friends.

'When Harry Met Sally...'

Interlude 1 – *faking it*

I'm not sure if it seems odd, or appropriate, that the woman who gave us the concept of the 'Single Girl' as 'the newest glamour girl of our age'[4] and *Cosmopolitan* magazine in its current, sexy, incarnation, thus helping kickstart the Swinging Sixties, would also eventually be responsible for promoting the idea that it was *polite* for women to fake orgasms. When Sally (Meg Ryan) devastates Harry (Billy Crystal) in 'Katz's' deli by making him suddenly doubt whether all the women he has slept with really have 'had an okay time', she is not only referencing a timeless open secret that, according to Nora Ephron all women know and no men want to consider, but also a topical idea within popular culture in the 1980s.

Helen Gurley Brown's breakthrough book, *Sex and the Single Girl*, was published in 1962, and she took over the then-ailing *Cosmopolitan* in 1965, boosting subscription rates and making it the first modern women's magazine dedicated to advice about sex *and* careers, clothes *and* politics. This stance that women's experiences should be limitless is echoed in the title of her 1982 bestseller, *Having It All: Love, Success, Sex, Money Even if You're Starting with Nothing*.[5] This is the kind of book Sally might pick up when browsing in 'Shakespeare and Co', a women's self-help manual, yet it advocates pleasing one's partner through deceit. Brown's earlier book boldly urged women to defy the 'double standard', the idea that men should be sexually experienced upon marriage, but their brides should be virgins. This defiance was radical enough for 1962, but the most outrageous part of her message was not just that 'nice girls do'[6] but that they should be prepared to admit it: 'Should a man think you are a virgin? I can't imagine why, if you aren't. Is he? Is there anything particularly attractive about a thirty-four-year old virgin?'[7]

By the time she was writing *Having It All* twenty years later, American societal assumptions, at least as represented in popular culture, had moved on enormously, thanks to the Pill, the sexual revolution and the women's movement. Brown's 1982 title implies her female readers do not have to compromise, to choose marriage and family *or* career success and money, which seems in keeping with the 1980s emphasis on self-advancement; but some of her notions seem more dated, even retrograde. Rather than insist that even respectable women enjoyed sex, as she had in her first book, Brown now downplayed the importance of sex to women, urging them to 'do it anyway' if their partners wanted to, adding ' You don't have to rev up and have an orgasm'.[8] Brown, once legible as a champion of women's sexual satisfaction, by this point was more intent to emphasise the primacy of male pleasure, male ego: 'After someone has made love to you with skill and grace, a [faked] orgasm is a way of saying you enjoyed yourself, even as you compliment your host on a wonderful spinach quiche.'[9]

Sally's deli sandwich may not be a spinach quiche but her exhibition underlines that, whether complimenting a successfully cooked meal or sexual performance, women's sincerity can be never assured.

Narrative Segment 1 – *context*

On the film's release, many reviewers, both positive and negative, remarked on its accurate reflection of the zeitgeist.[10] Although some disliked its 'yuppie' setting, it seems evident that part of Reiner and Ephron's intent in ensuring topicality was to establish a convincing contemporary milieu for the love story. This would then highlight both the departures and continuities in modern romance compared to the traditional romantic comedy. Situating Sally at a bookstore table with the latest self-help blockbusters reveals a tendency to rely on books for romantic guidance, establishing her emotional vulnerability more economically than several paragraphs of dialogue – even Ephron dialogue – could do. And making the books recent hits

would ensure nods of wry recognition from those who had seen the same titles themselves. The film has Harry read *The Icarus Agenda* for the same reasons Sally reads *Making Life Right When It Feels All Wrong*;[11] to illustrate their late 80s environment.

Assuming that the film was keen to be true to its time, then, the next question is, what time was that? In what context did *When Harry Met Sally...* arrive? What other films were big at the box office that year, what trends were obtaining generally in popular culture and beyond?

It is a conceit in popular history that if the 1970s were, as Tom Wolfe nicknamed them, the 'me decade',[12] the 80s were more the 'gimme decade'. The first title spoke to a general turning-inward in America, after the disillusionment of Watergate and Vietnam; reflecting a despair that government or society could be fixed, in the 70s the focus narrowed as individuals worked on understanding and improving themselves, a much smaller project with a greater prospect of success. I've noted elsewhere the effect this had on the contemporary romcom,[13] which began to include references to support groups and self-help manuals, like 1979's *Starting Over*, whose villain, the hero's selfish ex-wife, makes him leave the family home so that she can 'find herself'.

Marie and Sally amid topical bestsellers

Such introspective self-indulgence would come to seem old-fashioned in the next ten years; according to contemporary cinema, the people of the 'gimme decade' didn't want self-empowerment, they wanted money. This was the time when Gordon Gekko's (Michael Douglas) mantra, 'Greed is good', from *Wall Street* (1987) echoed Madonna's celebration of the 'Material Girl' (1984). Conspicuous consumption was in, along with shoulder pads and big hair. While this is very much a snapshot of the times filtered through then-popular culture, political and social historians have confirmed overt displays of materialism characterised the period; Nicolaus Mills, for example, suggests that the keynote of the era was sounded when Nancy Reagan wanted a new set of china – decorated with gold leaf and costing '$209, 508 for 220 place settings' – for her husband's inauguration as President in 1981.[14] While it might be reductive to see the decade's mores reflected in this one ostentatious gesture, Mills persuasively argues that the costly china was symbolic of the new American worldview ushered in under Reagan: 'American culture in the 1980s would be a culture based on triumph – on the admiration of power and status'.[15]

This urge towards triumphant *bigness* resulted in Hollywood in big special-effects movies and big franchises, repeated returns to products that had already proved themselves like the *Friday the Thirteenth* (1980–) and *Rocky* (1976–) series. Would-be serious, non-genre films looked at the current state of the nation, just as 70s films had, but instead of reproducing their pervasive paranoia and distrust of big business, government and state, there was a new respect for such institutions, an aspirational attitude towards them. In *Working Girl* (1988), for example, Tess McGill (Melanie Griffith) beats her treacherous 'bitch' boss in both business and romantic terms. Her ultimate reward is to *get* an office, not escape from one. When the camera pulls back from Tess in her new room, further and further back from the building, showing the sunlight glinting on hundreds of windows in hundreds of office blocks just like hers, the moment is supposed to be celebratory, not indicative of a hive filled with

indistinguishable drones. Similarly, the start of *Wall Street* shows streams of workers arriving for work in the financial district, pouring out of the subway and into office buildings, but unlike the similar images from, say, *Metropolis* (1927), where the number, similarity and anonymity of the workers is an indictment of the dystopia in which they live, *Wall Street* lacks any suggestion that there might be alienation in the massed ranks.

Against this culture of bigness, some writers and directors were managing to make personal pieces, and among them were Rob Reiner and Nora Ephron. Reiner, the son of director Carl Reiner and actress/singer Estelle, had started his career writing comedy and appearing in television shows from the late 60s; his role as Mike 'Meathead' Stivic in *All in the Family* (1971–9) became so identified with him that one review for *When Harry Met Sally...*, his fifth film, pigeonholed it as 'Meathead's Manhattan'. His first film, the mock-rockumentary *This Is Spinal Tap* (1984) was hailed as a comic success, and each of his subsequent forays into different genres was similarly well received.[16] *When Harry Met Sally...* was his most personal endeavour, however, since, as Reiner and Ephron have both acknowledged, not only was Harry Burns based on him, but the

Tess (Melanie Griffith, centre) is rewarded with a place in the hive (*Working Girl*, 1988)

impulse to make a film about the perils of the contemporary dating scene had arisen from Reiner's own experiences as a newly single man after his 1981 divorce.[17]

Ephron too had a history of working on personally inflected projects; although she saw herself primarily as a journalist,[18] her novel *Heartburn* (1983), a thinly veiled account of her husband's adultery and the resultant break-up of their marriage, had combined her signature sharp wit, interest in food and a portrait of the zeitgeist, elements that were to surface again in her screenplay for *When Harry Met Sally...* . Ephron has written that the movie's development was a long one, beginning with lunch meetings where Reiner and his friend, the film's producer, Andrew Scheinman, would shock her with tales from their dating life.[19]

In an earlier work on the development of the romantic comedy as a genre, I noted a tendency in other writings on the topic to gloss over the 80s:

Accounts ... often seem to compress the time between *Annie Hall* in 1977 and *When Harry Met Sally...* in 1989 [...] telescoping the twelve years between them into a single impulse began by Allen's film and adopted by Nora Ephron.[20]

Coming now to investigate the films that occupied that twelve-year gap, I realise the reasoning behind the common elision is simple: there were very few actual romcoms in that period. Between 1977, which gave audiences *Annie Hall* and *The Goodbye Girl*, and 1989, only a handful of films potentially qualified for inclusion in that genre, and then only if we are being liberal in its interpretation. The Dudley Moore vehicle, *10* (1979) is more of an adultery fantasy than a true romcom, while *Private Benjamin* (1980) is a depiction of a woman's self-discovery rather than a search for true love. Though there were many successful films featuring romance and comedy, such as 1983's *Tootsie* and 1984's *Romancing the Stone* and *Splash*, these films were not romantic comedies *per se*, but always had another more dominant element in their plots, such as masquerade, action and magic. Straightforward romcoms tended to be either about teens, as with 1984's *Sixteen Candles*, *The Sure Thing* in 1985 and the following year's *Pretty in Pink*, or only marginal hits at the box office: *Roxanne*, a reworking of the Cyrano de Bergerac story, managed only $17.6 million domestically in 1987.

There was definitely room for a blockbuster romantic comedy and while *Moonstruck* (1988) garnered an Oscar for Cher, it made only a respectable $34 million at the North American box office. *Working Girl*, in movie theatres from late 1988 into 1989 did better, with a $63 million domestic haul, but the $92.8 box office for *When Harry Met Sally...* underscores its phenomenal success, and indicates it tapped in to an audience hunger not only for films of this genre, but for innovative ones.

Screen International was not overly impressed by *When Harry Met Sally...* but was warm enough to imagine it worthy of a 'moderately successful run' in normal circumstances. It did not feel it would get these, however, given the competition at the box office: 'it's just too bad that Harry has to meet the likes of Batman and Indiana Jones as well'.[21] Although the summer release window was swamped with the usual big 80s films – not only *Batman* and *Indiana Jones and the Last Crusade*, but also a rash of sequels including *Lethal Weapon 2*, *Ghostbusters II* and *Back to the Future 2* – it is possible to see *When Harry Met Sally...* offering an escape from such action-filled pyrotechnics for audiences who would rather have a human-sized narrative set in the present day. These were rare: of the other top films of 1989, two were historically set mature dramas, *Driving Miss Daisy* and *Dead Poets Society*, while another two were comedy-sci-fi or comedy-fantasy hybrids, *Look Who's Talking* and *Honey, I Shrunk the Kids*. Only *Parenthood* out of the top ten seems located in the same real world as *When Harry met Sally...* and its emphasis on family and parenting troubles makes it more of a comedy drama.

What this swift overview of the filmic environment for *When Harry Met Sally...* exposes is that, although Ephron and Reiner were perceived as taking a risk with the small film, the time really was right for its release. While the director might worry that the film had 'no safety net at all'[22] since it only had its wit and warmth to recommend it, rather than a pre-sold product or even big box-office stars,[23] the extreme length of time that had passed since the last innovative romantic comedies should perhaps have allayed any fears. 1977's twin romcom bonanza garnered $38 million for *Annie Hall* and the excellent $102 million for *The Goodbye Girl*: twelve years later there were obviously audiences eager to see the same kind of story with equally winning performances.

Interlude 2 – *witnesses*

Nora Ephron's film work frequently demonstrates her familiarity with romcom tropes, her understanding of how they work and her willingness to subvert them playfully. *When Harry Met Sally...* displays these traits, not least in its ability to undermine the standard boy-meets-girl, boy-loses-girl, boy-gets-girl-back template through taking on the 'meet cute' convention and destabilising it by having the couple meet again and again. It is audacious, with Sally having driven away from Harry at the Washington Arch, to follow the couch couple's story with a shot of JFK airport and the surtitle: 'Five years

The film's first audacious leap in time

later'. How many romantic comedies are prepared to introduce their central couple and then apparently dissolve it for an interval of half a decade?

The film contrasts this lengthy, protracted relationship with the series of boy-meets-girl testimonials of successful meets cute, opposing Harry and Sally's story by featuring couples who fall in love at first sight, and forever. The structure that develops, with couch couples sections alternating with narrative sequences, is coherent, but not everyone at the time felt that it was successful, nor that the stories were genuinely derived. Indeed, the more censorious critics assumed these 'witness' sections were another 'bit' stolen from Woody Allen.

A couple of the reviewers[24] also noted that the testimonials were similar to equivalent moments in Warren Beatty's *Reds* (1981), a political epic about two American journalists, John Reed (Beatty) and Louise Bryant (Diane Keaton), caught up in the Russian revolution. A closer consideration reveals a more complex story. While Allen had shown characters directly addressing the camera before *Reds* did, his early uses of the technique were different; for example, *Take the Money and Run* (1969) is a mock documentary where the speakers deliver information about the notorious criminal, Virgil Starkwell, played by Allen himself. *Annie Hall* used the direct address when Alvy (Allen again) and other characters occasionally stepped out of scenes to talk to the viewer about the events occurring on screen, as in the famous Marshall McLuhan scene. But *Reds* made a different use of the device. Beatty's movie starts with fifteen short witness statements, made direct to camera by people who *really* knew the actual Bryant and Reed. In all, thirty-two interviewees discuss the personalities and actions of Bryant and Reed. At 194 minutes, the film is epic in both length and ambition, and with an earnestness about political matters that made it ripe for mockery.

Allen appears to have been prepared to indulge in this, as his *Zelig* (1983) repurposes the witness idea, introducing real-life contemporary celebrities such as Susan Sontag and Saul Bellow, but having them discuss the life and actions of a made-up character, not

only resolutely non-heroic, but even a non-person: Leonard Zelig (Allen again), the human chameleon, a man so utterly without personality that he takes on the attributes of the people with whom he comes into contact.

If Allen appropriated the 'witnesses' trope for *Zelig*, he was doing so perhaps to send up the rather humourless *Reds*, perhaps because that film – and Beatty himself – borrowed Diane Keaton, Allen's own former girlfriend and star, or perhaps because *Reds* in

Zelig's 'witnesses' (1983)

turn had stolen Allen's jazz and black-and-white credits – a point for which critics would later attack Reiner and Ephron but forgive Beatty. The film-makers of *When Harry Met Sally...* then could be seen not simply stealing from Allen with the couch couple format, but being involved in a dense network of allusions and borrowings among movies and movie personnel.

Like Allen, Ephron and Reiner do not have witnesses to heroic deeds, but rather to ordinary if romantic stories, but more like Beatty they employ this chorus at one remove from the main characters of the narrative. Whatever the inspiration – personal or allusive or both – the couch couple segments, like many aspects of *When Harry Met Sally...* have had a lasting impact on the romcom. Romantic comedy-cum-action thriller *Mr. & Mrs. Smith* (2005) turns the couple confessional into a session with a marriage therapist, taking the

The dysfunctional couch couple (Brad Pitt and Angelina Jolie, *Mr. & Mrs. Smith*, 2005); the re-enamoured couch couple initially adversarial nature of Harry and Sally's relationship and putting it on the couch with a professional counsellor, the pair's gradual rapprochement legible in their demeanour and costumes. This was an evolution of the trope that was continued in, for example, *What Happens in Vegas* (2008). There Joy (Cameron Diaz) and Jack (Ashton Kutcher) take the accustomed sides of the couch, man on the left, woman on the right; though the narrative shows them ostensibly loathing each other, the fact that they spontaneously say the same thing indicates they are right for each other after all, just as Harry and Sally's simultaneous actions and words had done twenty years earlier.

Narrative Segment 2 – *couch couples*

While contemporary reviewers were swift to assume the direct-to-camera stories of husbands and wives in these interludes were a notion 'borrowed' from Woody Allen, both Reiner and Ephron have declared their origin was more personal. In both commentaries on the DVDs (2001, 2008), the director relates how he heard a friend's father talking about how he met his wife, and was struck by how animated the older man became reminiscing about this.

Reiner's realisation that all married people would have a similar special story made him decide to incorporate such tales in the romantic comedy. Ephron, in the 2008 commentary, adds that the story of the future partners who first see each other at summer camp is her *own* parents' meet cute. While, then, the couch couple segments are filmed with actors, the stories themselves are asserted, by director and writer, to be true, and included for personal reasons.

There are seven instances of the couch couple scene, all shot in the same way, on the same sofa, the man on screen left and the woman on screen right, the speakers directly addressing the camera. Although variously humorous and touching, these scenes do more than merely entertain while establishing the importance of romantic coupledom: each also introduces significant themes and tropes that

Six couch couples form the 'witnesses' in *When Harry Met Sally…*

relate to Harry and Sally's story, sometimes as a forecast of action about to happen, sometimes casting back to the previous narrative sequence.

The first couple sequence, for example, features a man relating how he was sitting in a restaurant – 'A Horn and Hardart Cafeteria' – when a beautiful woman walked in. He told his friend he was going to marry that girl, and two weeks later he did. They have been married for over fifty years, he proudly finishes. The testimonial's position at the start of the film is not random; it, rather than any of the other stories, has been carefully chosen to begin the picture, as it establishes several key ideas and elements of the movie to come. Within its brief run-time, it introduces smaller recurrent tropes – the friend, the restaurant – as well as the bigger themes of longevity and spontaneity. Harry and Sally will be shown talking to their friends about their relationship with each other; diners and restaurants are the settings for certain significant moments. Tacitly, too, the locale of New York City is hinted at, or at least an urban milieu like New York, since the most famous of the 'Horn and Hardart Cafeterias' was there.

Most importantly, this first couple scene establishes the significance of *time*: it is going to be crucial to the story of the other eventual couple whose names figure in the film's title. The older man and woman symbolise two of the most common romantic comedy clichés, love at first sight and loving forever, but attest that these clichés exist in real life too – they happened to them. This sets up an important contrast with our future couple, Harry and Sally, because they very evidently do *not* fall in love at first sight: unlike the man and his wife here, they do not know they are meeting 'the one' at their first encounter. While this man and wife seem to love both immediately and lastingly, the only aspect of longevity in Harry and Sally's relationship we see is the length of time it takes them to get together.

If the first couple's story introduced the key concept of *time*, the second's presents the importance of *separation*. As the man and woman confide, they were high-school sweethearts at sixteen, but

WHEN HARRY MET SALLY... | 25

then his family moved away. They did not meet again for thirty-four years, but when they did, 'it was just as though not a single day had gone by'. What is significant is that their love has endured despite the time apart. Since this segment precedes our main couple's next meeting five years after their farewells by the Washington Arch, the idea that an attraction can persist is reassuring.

The scene strikes one other meaningful keynote: the man relates that he was walking down Broadway when he re-encountered his former girlfriend. This underlines the fact that New York City is *the* place where love happens. Confirming that the place to which Sally and Harry have just driven is not the impersonal urban jungle the audience might fear, but a place where coincidence can bring back one's long lost love, this sequence provides helpful pointers for the next scene: lovers may part, but the passage of time can bring them together again, especially in a place like New York.

The third testimonial features a couple that does not seem close and affectionate, thus introducing the notion of *conflict*, which is paramount to the initial relations between Sally and Harry. This husband and wife reveal that they have been married and divorced and remarried. This time the sequence doesn't mention New York City landmarks, but it does return to the importance of time, via the thirty-five years between their wedding days. Positioning this sequence right after Sally and Harry's less-than-friendly encounter in the airport is significant because it assures us not only that love can triumph, even over many years and despite surface frictions, but that, if people are fated to be together, they will be eventually, even if one of them marries someone else in the interim. As Harry is about to marry Helen (Harley Kozak), this assertion is comforting as it allows us to believe that our central protagonists will finally fall in love.

Each of the couch couple segments has something to contribute to Harry and Sally's unfolding story, whether it is a forecast of similar outcomes in the future or the introduction of a symbolic element that will become significant. What the fourth segment supplies is the notion that proximity is not enough to make a couple: there has to be fate as well. The man and woman in the fourth testimonial relate that, although they were born, lived and worked near each other in New York City, they did not meet until both were on visits to Chicago. This segment underlines that being in the same vicinity does not guarantee the finding of one's true love. In the case of this couple, it seems as if fate took a hand in it, finally arranging their meeting when their daily routines failed to help them connect.

It is obviously no coincidence that the two cities they mention are the two most significant to the Harry and Sally story; as the next narrative segment goes on to explore, even though our two protagonists have met, live in New York now, and are both single, this is not sufficient to turn them into a couple. Fate must play a part too. The alternation now between narrative and testimonial sequences acquires some suspense, as we wait for something to change the status quo.

As the film progresses, the protagonists move gradually nearer and nearer to forming a romantic couple; after the enjoyably frustrating *almost but not quite* quality of the New Year's Eve scene, where Harry and Sally recognise their own growing attraction to each other, we might hope that the fifth couch segment will provide more hints of their union. The scene we get, however, does not at first glance deliver this. This testimonial story is so divergent from Sally and Harry's experiences it seems almost to suggest that they have no hope of getting together.

Again we have the same setting with the same positioning of the man and woman, here with their outfits, in traditionally contrasting blue and pink, underlining their gender. Their story, related this time almost entirely by the woman, is also traditional, involving balance and symmetry. The woman tells how she and her future husband met when they were both counsellors at summer camps. They met at a dance after he had come over and introduced himself; she had assumed he was coming to talk to her friend Maxine. The man says his name on cue, as his wife gets to that part of the story, and her response is both touching and humorous: 'At that moment I knew, I knew the way you know about a good melon'. Nora Ephron has said that this is her parents' meeting story: with the comic emphasis on food, this analogy seems appropriate, given Ephron's own obsession with the topic.

This interlude sets up a strong contrast with our protagonists: while instinct tells the woman she belongs with the man, Harry and Sally have not recognised each other as the right partners. Two hints are there, however, that this story has a positive parallel with that of Sally and Harry: the mention of food and the significance of the woman's friend. Food scenes are important to *When Harry Met Sally...* and Sally, in particular, is portrayed as extremely discriminating about her choices, from menu options in restaurants to individual tomatoes at a grocery salad bar. The fact that the woman in this scene invokes a critical appraisal of food as a comparison to her instant feeling actually does bode well for Sally. Exercising careful if instinctive judgment need not disbar her from romantic happiness.

Friend Maxine is also a significant part of the story. When the woman relates with visible satisfaction that her man did not come across the room to talk to Maxine, but to *her*, the importance of rivalry for a potential partner is introduced. This introduces the idea of assuming someone is interested in one's companion, which fits nicely with the subsequent narrative scene, where Harry and Sally try to defuse their growing attraction for each other by setting one another up with their *other* best friends, Jess (Bruno Kirby) and Marie (Carrie Fisher). The narrative segment that follows briefly and comically establishes Jess and Marie as a latterday couple worthy of their seat on the couch: they meet and seem to know at once, like the other testimonial pairs, that they are meant to be together. When, at the end of the segment, Jess and Marie escape their stilted evening as a foursome to be alone together, it may feel a little soon for another couch sequence. Although it does diverge from the timing if not the structure already established, there are a couple of significant reasons that make it an appropriate fit here.

The couple this sixth time consists of a man and his wife from China; the man narrates that the woman was suggested as a suitable bride by a marriage-arranger but he did not want to agree until he had seen her, so went to her village to peek at his potential wife. Importantly, he says this is because he 'wanted to make sure'. Seeing her and thinking she looked nice, he agreed, and they married – and have been together for fifty-five years.

This scene re-emphasises some key ideas from the couch segments; the idea of a married relationship lasting forever, and, as the man's comment about wanting to know whether she was the right one indicates, there is also the idea that *seeing* his future partner would help him judge. The story can thus be viewed as a parallel of Jess and Marie's, apart from the rejection of the original suggested mate, because the notion of the arranging of a marriage is obviously crucial here too. Just as Jess and Marie are each set up by their friends, one look tells them what they need to know about their right partners, and in the next sequence of scenes, this leads to marriage. The comedy inherent in Jess and Marie's rejection of their intended dates in favour of each other does not undermine the fact that they choose each other – we could say *recognise* each other, since it seems so rapid – as their proper future spouses.

The satisfying regularity ensured by the repetition of alternating the couples' testimonials with narrative sections about our protagonists is suspended about two thirds of the way through the film; the Chinese couple's story is thus the last one before the protagonists themselves finally graduate to the couch and make it clear that we have been watching their meeting (and re-meeting, and re-meeting) story. Unlike the half-minute narratives provided by the older couples, it has taken Sally and Harry around ninety minutes to encompass *their* union. But at last they give us the longed-for happy ending.

Not only does the brief sequence with Sally and Harry on the couch confirm them as perfect partners like the other married couples, and seem to forecast for them an equally long and devoted marriage, it also recaps some of the main elements and key terms from the previous testimonial sequences, thus providing a gratifying sense of conclusion augmenting the satisfaction of the romcom genre's need for coupled closure. Their playful bickering is an echo of the *conflict* that has bedevilled their relationship since their first meeting. The important, opposing, tropes of *spontaneity* and *longevity* are evoked here too, via the brief three months they waited to get married once together, and the long twelve years it took to get them to that point. The description of the wedding cake confirms the significance that *food* choices and eating together have played in the narrative, while the emphasis on their friendship links to the testimonial stories about matchmaking, being chosen instead of one's friend, and, above all, to the avowed driving question of the film, emblazoned on its posters, 'Can two friends sleep together and still love each other in the morning?'

Interlude 3 – *montage*

One of my favourite sections of the movie comes at the start of the fourth narrative segment; Harry and Sally have finally agreed to be friends, and the sequence shows Harry in particular grieving for his marriage. In this film of extremely clever design, the scene has one of the most interesting and complex structures of all, in which we simultaneously *see* a succession of disconnected images, but *hear* a complete phone conversation between Harry and Sally – not shown until the final part of the segment. This creates a tightly composed, elegantly efficient montage illustrating the passing of time as the two get to know each other and start to heal emotionally.

Throughout the first part of the sequence, while the image/soundtracks are not aligned, a slow, stripped-down piano rendition of 'But Not for Me' is heard underneath the dialogue. This aptly reflects Harry's worldview, as he seems particularly depressed about his split from Helen, and the downbeat lyrics reflect his pessimistic personality. While visuals depict the two protagonists going about their daily lives – noticeably with Harry passively staring into space,

Moments from the 'grieving' montage: Harry's passive
depression contrasts with Sally's active recuperation

Sally more actively pursuing interests – the sound of a late-night phone call reveals their growing intimacy. When Harry calls her, Sally is watching *Casablanca* (1942) again, and he immediately turns on his television too. This reference back to the first film they discussed and the fact that they now agree about the ending, shows how far they have come in their friendship, while also indicating, since it attracts no comment, how frequent late-night calls, and watching TV together in their different apartments, have become.

As they watch *Casablanca* together, they feel free to talk over it until its famous ending; their conversation, with Harry allowing his hypochondria free rein and repeating how much he misses his ex-wife, flows over the film that is not yet visible to the viewer and also the various images that are. One shows Harry alone, reading a book, with a thermometer in his mouth and other health paraphernalia at his side. True to his boast to Sally ten years ago, he is still reading the last page of a new book first, in case he dies before he gets a chance to finish it. Appropriately, the novel is Stephen King's *Misery* (1987), and this text actually has resonances beyond its apposite title: its status as a contemporaneous bestseller bolsters the film's topical feel but also, more covertly, the book functions as an in-joke for cast and crew as the film version of *Misery* was Reiner's next directorial project.

At this point, Sally's voice is heard exclaiming, 'Last scene'. The visuals now align with the audio track, but the sequence has not finished with its more experimental composition: instead of cutting from Sally's apartment to Harry's and back again, with each shot showing one of them watching their favourite movie, a split-screen technique shows both simultaneously. Furthermore, the split has been arranged so that the two appear as if they are lying in the same bed. The camera is positioned behind them so we see their heads together, seemingly on one pillow.

The use of split-screen here not only shows the friends in an unwittingly intimate position that forecasts their eventual union as a couple, but also acts as another instance of the cinephilia observable throughout *When Harry Met Sally...* . While contemporary reviewers

mainly assumed that the split-screen device was borrowed from Woody Allen's *Annie Hall*, the juxtaposition of Harry and Sally in bed seems to owe more to famous battle-of-the-sexes comedies *Indiscreet* (1958) or *Pillow Talk* (1959), the latter playfully juxtaposing career girl Jan Morrow (Doris Day) with playboy Brad Allen (Rock Hudson).

Annie Hall employs the split-screen tactic twice, once to show the differences between Annie's (Diane Keaton) staid WASP household and Alvy's noisy Jewish one, and the other, most famously, contrasting the pair's analysis sessions: it is no coincidence that on both occasions Alvy gets two thirds of the screen while Annie is relegated to the remaining

Split-screen: *Indiscreet* (1958) juxtaposes Philip (Cary Grant) and Anna (Ingrid Bergman) in their beds; *Pillow Talk* (1959) uses the split-screen to imply mixed bathing

portion.[25] The equable split between Harry and Sally, however, maintains its focus on both of them and here borrows the sex comedy's techniques, as Reiner and Ephron acknowledge in the 2004 DVD commentary. Examination of the *Indiscreet* scene shows how Ephron at least was influenced directly by the Cary Grant film: Grant and *Casablanca*'s Ingrid Bergman are positioned in their own single beds in such a way that the split-screen unites them in a double, just as Harry and Sally are united in the similar shots. And, just as the double bed image forecasts the eventual resolution of the older film with Grant

Harry and Sally watch television alone but together; in *Annie Hall* (1977) the split-screen gives more space to him (Woody Allen) than her (Diane Keaton)

and Bergman as a couple, so *When Harry Met Sally...* assures viewers of its own happy ending.

With the split-screen device established, we then see the friends watching *Casablanca*; some of the movie's dialogue can be heard as the TV screens show Ingrid Bergman's luminous face. This is the cue for some of Harry's relationship shtik, his notion of high- and low-maintenance women. It is typical of him to try to classify people by their gender and behaviour in such an inflexible, even if humorous, way. As Harry explains his taxonomy, the camera set-up reverses, so that the friends are now shown face on; again their beds are arranged so that, though separate, the sizes and heights align so they look as if they are sharing a kingsize divan. But as this discussion comes to an end, a cut takes us back to the shots of the backs of their heads as they watch the film, crucially at its denouement, since it allows us, with them, to witness the very end, in which Rick announces to his new ally the police chief, that 'I think this is the beginning of a beautiful friendship'. The analogy is pointed enough, but Harry underlines its significance: 'Ooh, best last line of a movie, ever'. The two are enjoying their own 'beautiful friendship' very much at this moment.

As Sally sighs happily at *Casablanca*'s poignant conclusion, the angle on the pair switches so that they are facing the camera again.

Harry and Sally are linked by telephone, as in earlier romantic comedies ...

Sally now begins to get ready for sleep, while trying to reassure her pessimistic friend that he does not have some new disease. Sally asks him if he will be able to sleep, rolling her eyes and laughing a little as Harry retorts that, if not, he will lie there moaning, and begins to practise. But very significantly, when they finally, simultaneously, hang up their phones, and even when she eventually turns out her light, the dual screen is maintained, Harry in his half – on the lefthand screen when we are looking at them face on, just like the men in the couch sequences – remaining in his portion of the screen rather than claiming it all. This is a departure from the sex comedies' use of the split-screen device, where the dual screens were conjured, and banished, by the picking up and putting down of the telephone receiver. This serves to suggest that more than just telephone lines connect Harry and Sally; they share an awareness of each other's physical presence – out there somewhere in the city – even when not directly in contact. The mutuality of this awareness accounts for the simultaneity with which they hang up, and underlines their closeness.

Narrative Segment 3 – *music*

Although at the start of both DVD commentaries, director Rob Reiner claims that incorporating jazz classics into film soundtracks

... but their connection persists even when they hang up

was not common when he included the fifteen standards in *When Harry Met Sally...*, as we will see later, the music was one of the main elements reviewers felt had been stolen from Woody Allen. One opined that Reiner 'picked musical selections in the crudest possible way', unlike Allen, whose scores had 'a life as full and rich as any of the characters'.[26] The notion of appropriating elements from Allen films will be examined later; the music itself will be explored now as it is so integral to *When Harry Met Sally...* .

Quite contrary to the reviewer above, I find the Reiner–Ephron film surpasses the Allen romcoms in its employment of music. Reiner may have been disingenuous asserting that he initiated movie use of jazz classics, but it is evident that the film utilises such songs in a much more sophisticated way than Allen. Where the music just *accompanies* events in *Annie Hall* and *Manhattan*, in *When Harry Met Sally...*, it comments on, undercuts or underlines them. For example, the Gershwin song, 'Strike up the Band', played at the end of *Manhattan* (1979) simply underscores the scene in which Isaac Davis (Woody Allen) runs across town to find his former lover: there is no subtext, the song's lyrics are not being evoked, the orchestral version simply matches the song's rapid tempo to the protagonist's speedy movement.

By contrast, the music and songs in *When Harry Met Sally...* are carefully deployed to ironic effect, for added pathos, to emphasise covert emotions, as part of the film's cinephilia, and sometimes several of these at once. Above all, their function is to convey or comment on *Harry's* feelings. Overwhelmingly, when a tune accompanies a scene that only Sally is in, the music is actually being played aloud where she is – it is diegetic. The music that predominates, however, is non-diegetic, music that is not in the world of the action but can be interpreted as reflecting characters' moods – *Harry's* moods. Sally indeed is permitted only one instance of non-diegetic music, which accompanies the second time she is seen buying and moving a Christmas tree. Given her unhappiness at the pointed contrast with the previous occasion she bought one, with Harry, the use of 'Have Yourself a Merry Little Christmas' is ironically at odds with her state of mind.

This conscious play with diegetic/non-diegetic music persists throughout. At times, a song moves from being on the soundtrack into the world of the film – as with the first tune in the narrative sections. 'Our Love Is Here to Stay' by George and Ira Gershwin, in a Louis Armstrong recording, provides an ironic commentary in the first narrative scene; as Armstrong describes the permanence of his love, Harry and Amanda (Michelle Nicastro) are saying goodbye; he will try to replace her with Sally within the day, and soon forget her entirely. The music is sardonically contrasting the lasting love enshrined in romantic classic songs and Harry's shallow feelings. Sally's part in the rupture of their romance is also signalled; although the tune is heard before her arrival, it then becomes what she is playing in her car; when she cuts off the song mid-line, interrupting the lyrics, it forecasts how she will soon interrupt Harry's feelings about Amanda.

The film continues to use the standards, occasionally in a straightforward manner, as when Christmas songs accompany seasonal scenes, but typically in more sly ways to elucidate Harry's emotions; at the start of the airport scene, when the protagonists meet again after five years, the accompanying music is the Rodgers and Hart song 'Where or When'. Since Harry 'can't remember where or when' they have met before, the tune is comically appropriate, but also, by being a romantic classic, again provides support for the notion that he and Sally will get together by the film's end.

Schematic use of non-diegetic music for Harry, either when he is alone or with Sally, continues throughout the narrative. The tune 'Don't Be That Way' is played at the wedding when he is trying to overcome Sally's frostiness; 'But Not for Me' is heard, fittingly, twice when Harry is feeling lonely. Significantly, the second time this tune is used, on New Year's Eve, the film cuts between the plaintive non-diegetic tune that matches Harry's feelings, and the played-out-loud music at the party where Sally is. The ironic commentary set up by the clash between Sally's moods and the music, noted with the Christmas song above, continues in this instance, as she is hearing 'Isn't It Romantic?' while being assailed by a man telling her a dirty joke.

On two occasions songs feature overtly in the narrative, and both provide further subtle hints of Harry's feelings. He happily uses 'a singing machine' when shopping in 'The Sharper Image', enjoying his own rendition of 'The Surrey with the Fringe on Top' from *Oklahoma!* (1955). It is noticeable that in his gleeful singing and acting out Harry takes the role of Curley, and by serenading her, puts Sally into the role of Laurie, another indication that the pair will end up forming a couple, just as Curley and Laurie in the musical. At the end of the film, when he is trying to reconcile with Sally, Harry is seen with the same machine in his apartment. He has gone out and bought the gadget to serenade her again. The song with which he now regales Sally is aptly entitled 'Call Me', which is what he wants her to do, but it also has further significant lyrics. Harry is seemingly not yet ready to admit he loves Sally, perhaps to himself as well as to her, and thus changes the line 'Tell the one who loves you only' to 'Tell the one who *digs* you only'. The fact that he makes the substitution, however, plays up the changed word and underlines its significance.

While not all audience members will be familiar with every song or lyric, or even realise that such things are being consciously employed to add to the movie's meaning, it is evident that such musical choices have been made with great care and used for different effects. It is satisfying that the same attention given to selecting traditional tracks is also devoted to choosing 70s songs for the first diner scene. Not only are they historically appropriate: as 1970s pop, they represent the kind of song that would be played on a diner's jukebox. But the tracks also humorously illustrate Harry's changing moods: as he disparages Sheldon, the background song is the Allman Brothers' 'Ramblin' Man', a paean to the type of freewheeling masculinity Harry likes to imagine he possesses himself.

And later, as Harry stares contemplatively at her, his desire to seduce Sally is inspired by the sensual tones of Jennifer Warnes crooning: 'It's the Right Time of the Night (for Making Love)'.

Apart from the musical selections functioning to underscore emotions, or contrast with them, *When Harry Met Sally...* also utilises the older Hollywood trope of the musical motif, giving the couple a recurring love theme. This is the romantic Jones and Kahn classic 'It Had to Be You', which wraps around the film's entire structure. A light, uptempo piano version accompanies the opening credits, and Harry Connick, Jr sings it while the end credits roll. It plays when Harry and Sally walk through Central Park after their third meeting, deciding to become friends. After they have sex, the theme emerges again as Harry sits miserably in bed; this time the tune has a slow, plaintive piano treatment, and, significantly, the scene finishes without the music being allowed to resolve. The discordant effect this creates illustrates how their relationship has been disrupted by the sex, or at least by Harry's reaction to it.

It is apt, then, that the song is heard in its most lush treatment, with swelling orchestra and vocals by Frank Sinatra, at the moment of Harry's epiphany: *it has to be Sally*. The complex cutting of the following scene, with Harry rushing to be with her, and Sally trying to leave the party, shows via the use of music how the pair are bound together emotionally. Before, feeling sorry for himself, Harry's scenes had one tune playing under events, while Sally was hearing others actually played at the party; now the rush of his emotional revelation joins them across space: 'It Had to Be You' is heard in both their separate scenes and locales, diegetic and non-diegetic fusing as the lovers' worlds are united.

While some critics were quick to note and disparage as blatant copying the presence of the jazz standards, including this one, *and* the use of *Casablanca*, as will be discussed below, none linked these, yet 'It Had to Be You' was sung by Dooley Wilson in the 1942 film. Given the significance the classic film has to Harry and Sally, as something they first argue over, then watch together, the employment of this song can hardly be coincidental, but underlines the film-makers' cinephilia.

So, although contemporary reviewers linked the use of jazz classics to Woody Allen, it seems clear that *When Harry Met Sally...*, if using the same generic material, is doing so in a much more complex way. It employs the romantic standards most often to illustrate or undercut the moods and emotions of the male protagonist. Can we see this as a further indication of Sally's pragmatism and Harry's self-image as an interestingly tortured individual? She hears real music; he has a fitting (or mocking) soundtrack generated for him by the film.

Interlude 4 – *shtik*

One of the film's many pleasures is that it has been so skilfully composed that moments threatening to become too emotional are succeeded by lighter, humorous ones, which stop the mood becoming too sombre. Admittedly, not everyone admired these adroit changes of tone:

Where the film falls short is in Reiner's unwillingness to let emotional truth remain on the screen for more than a fleeting moment. Nearly every time a scene threatens to turn dark or unpleasant, Reiner chooses to 'rescue' it with a joke or gag.[27]

Two things occur to me in response to this; first, that Reiner is not necessarily to blame here, because he is following Ephron's script, which, as a comedy, would tend to avoid the dark and unpleasant; second, I wonder if it is not the film deflecting emotion, so much as the character of Harry. Other reviewers had noted a similar facet in Crystal, suggesting he possessed 'a hooded facility'[28] or, as *Newsweek* put it: 'he's too cool and self-protective an actor to work as a romantic leading man; we want to see the inner life behind the shtik'.[29]

It seems to me that these criticisms of Crystal are actually comments on the character he is playing. Harry's humour is based on his verbal facility, his wiseguy patter; frequently he employs this to defuse an emotional situation. For example, when Harry and Sally meet for the second time on the plane journey, he announces to her surprise that he is getting married. When she congratulates him, he undercuts her pleasure at his optimism, by implying he is marrying from fatigue with 'the whole life of a single guy thing'. His resultant monologue about dating is funny but reveals his selfishness and, again, his belief in the fundamental difference of the two sexes.

Though his comic patter is driven by the urge to win her over, we can now start to recognise it as his shtik. This is probably where we become aware for the first time that comic 'bits' like this, the monologue, are something he *does*. Harry is a funny guy, but the problem is he knows it. However, what becomes apparent is that he uses humour to deflect attention from his feelings. He could therefore be using it here to disguise how much he loves Helen: the comic patter is designed to project a nonchalance quite at odds with his emotional investment in his relationship.

Harry's comic repartee is on show again in a later scene, brought to life by Billy Crystal's excellent skills of timing and improvisation, when the two stroll through Central Park. The joke about combining newspaper real estate and obituary columns is quintessential Harry: witty, but with a dark undertone. This is in perfect keeping with his gloomy take on life, but instead of parading his existential angst, as he did ten years earlier, Harry now submerges it in a jocular remark, making Sally laugh: both are maturing.

Harry's shtik gets three more significant outings: the most ill-fated is when he mentions the idea of 'dog years' when trying to make up with Sally at the wedding, but his patter only succeeds in infuriating her further. Later, when he tries to reconcile with her by constantly calling her, we hear him leaving a message on her answerphone. Harry asks her to pick up, as he 'really wants to talk to' her but, just as she looks tempted, he again undermines the emotion in his plea by resorting to comic patter. The camera dwells for a moment on Sally's face as she listens, looking sad, then rolls her

eyes at his inexorable impulse to make a joke of things when he is
feeling vulnerable.

The final instance of Harry's shtik occurs after he has finally
confessed his love to Sally and secured her embrace. Harry brings
them both down from this rapture by commenting on the words to
'Auld Lang Syne', and again this prompts the usual eye-roll from
Sally, but she has learned to endure his patter now, and cleverly turns
his deflection comment back to their relationship with her line about
old friends.

Harry's shtik ...; ... and Sally's reaction

Much of the comedy is derived from Harry's one-liners and smart remarks, convincingly and hilariously performed by Crystal, but the character of Harry is endowed with sufficient depth for the viewer to realise that his humour is often a defence mechanism, that occasionally threatens to lose Harry the woman he loves.

Narrative Segment 4 – *'symmetry and recurrence'*

I have mentioned before that one of the film's key pleasures is its carefully organised structure. Even critics who were mostly negative about the film appreciated this, with *7 Days* confirming: 'The scenario is full of symmetry and recurrence',[30] and *The Village Voice* remarking on the film working 'by reprises, choric refrains'.[31] Indeed it is designed around paired or matching moments either in different sequences across the film, or within specific scenes. In this section, I want to take a look at some of these symmetries and reprises as they work in the longer sequences of the movie, the main building blocks of the narrative.

Diner scenes

When, wrong-footed by Harry's deadpan assumption of her sexual inexperience, Sally stumbles into the diner protesting the reverse, she

Ryan expertly performs Sally's embarrassment

manages to announce to the entire restaurant that she *has* had plenty of good sex. Meg Ryan performs Sally's mortification extremely effectively: we can tell how embarrassed Sally is by the extreme angle at which she holds her head while she walks to their table, an angle which shields her from having to make eye contact with any of the diners to whom she has just made this intimate declaration. This incident obviously forecasts, and indeed results in, the more famous diner scene later in the movie; there Sally exacts her revenge on Harry for the humiliation he has caused her here by embarrassing him in return.

For this matched moment, in one of the most famous scenes in recent cinema, one interlude has already considered the context of the faked orgasm and another will look at parodies of it, so what else can one say of a scene that has become such a part of contemporary popular culture that even people who have never seen *When Harry Met Sally...* can recite the punchline? One thing to acknowledge is the collaborative nature of the scene's genesis. As Reiner and Ephron make equally clear, both they and the two actors made contributions to its creation.[32] Ephron states that Reiner and Scheinman, having appalled her with their revelations of men's secrets, wanted to hear whether women did similar things.[33] In addition to admitting that women sometimes send themselves flowers, which found its way into Marie's story, Ephron revealed that women sometimes faked orgasms. Scheinman and Reiner loved the idea of incorporating this into the film and wrote a speech for Sally to deliver, but it was Ryan who suggested she actually act it out, 'somewhere incongruous'.[34] The famous punchline was then suggested by Crystal, and delivered in impeccably dry style by Estelle Reiner, the director's mother.

The deli scene echoes and balances out the earlier diner moment, as this time Sally is in full control of the situation, wilfully attracting attention and getting revenge on Harry. In both cases *he* is the bystander and *she* is the active one. In the former instance, she is embarrassed, but in the latter, it is her choice to make a scene, and smugly teach him a lesson.

The scene begins with Sally enquiring about Harry's avoidance of post-intercourse intimacy, and announcing that she is pleased she never got involved with him because she would inevitably end up as just another one of the women he left at 3 am. This statement is enlightening as it reveals that she wants more from Harry than a one-night stand. He can see that she is angry, but fails to realise that this is tantamount to a declaration of her feelings for him. When he says 'This is not about you', and she retorts 'Yes it *is*!' she is saying as clearly as she can at this point that being his friend is no longer

The two diner scenes

enough. Sally, however, hides the avowal by burying her personal anger in feminine solidarity: he is 'an affront to all women'. But it seems the resultant punishment by embarrassment is *not only* to pay him back for her discomfiture in the earlier diner scene, and *not only* for his hubris at thinking himself a phenomenal lover, but *also* because she is jealous of him sleeping with other women.

Besides Meg Ryan's spirited performance, three more aspects of the scene illustrate why it is such a satisfying one to watch. First, Harry's supreme sexual confidence is carefully established by Crystal's decision to carry on eating while talking with Sally about his escape habits, though she slaps her sandwich down in annoyance: this precisely demonstrates Harry's nonchalance about his behaviour, and suggests he equates sex with food, a hunger for both being frequently aroused and simply assuaged. The other two micro-moments bookend Sally's faking performance: Ryan conveys the moment Sally decides to teach him a lesson by a slight sideways look of her eyes, as if weighing something up, along with a tiny jutting motion of her jaw. She then goes into her exhibition, moaning, banging the table, tossing her head from side to side and attracting the attention of the other diner patrons. When she has finished, she breathes deeply once and then picks up her fork again, smiles at

Harry is dismissive

Sally decides to teach him a lesson ... fakes it ... and then cheerfully returns to her lunch

Harry and calmly takes a bite of food. The return to normal lunch behaviour is evidence that she was putting on a show for him as, her actions imply, other women will have done. She considers her point proven. And it seems as if she is right, since, miraculously, for once Harry has nothing to say – he just smiles sheepishly. Of course any response from him is made unnecessary because of the riposte from Estelle Reiner, but denying Harry the last word feels like a victory for Sally here.

Sex dream/fantasy

These paired moments grant us further insights into the characters of the protagonists. Harry's story sounds more like one of his comic routines than an actual dream, and underlines that though he is maturing, he still looks on sex as a competitive sport – and one at which he considers himself to be Olympic-standard. This vaunted expertise will be undermined in the celebrated deli scene, but for now Harry is left to boast, again revealing his fundamental belief in the differences between the desires of men and of women. His throwaway punchline, 'Must've been the dismount', links back to his conversation with Sally when he asserted all men wanted to leave straight after sex. Crudely the *dismount* can be taken as the moment when he rolls off his prone partner, but metaphorically it is the moment when he tries to disengage from intimacy and depart.

Sally's fantasy is similarly illuminating, but about her lack of an adult sex drive and imagination, rather than lack of commitment. Comically, Harry again manages to get her to recount her fantasy, even though she thinks it's embarrassing, by telling her *not* to tell him. She then relates her desire for a faceless man to rip off her clothes. Nothing else happens in this fantasy, which is pointedly lacking both in detail and in actual sex. It is the run-up, rather than the act, which Sally thinks about, or rather the *costuming*, since the only variable element in the fantasy is what she is wearing. These symmetrical scenes demonstrate not only how comfortable the friends now are with each other, but also that they belong together.

Sex with Harry will show Sally just what she has been missing, increase her satisfaction with her sex life, while committing to Sally will be a sign of maturity in Harry. He will give the faceless man an identity, as she will help him with his dismount problem.

Win, lose or draw

The famous 'Baby Fish Mouth!' scene seems so naturalistic that it would be tempting to assume it was entirely improvised, but this would be to overlook the skill involved in its construction. The DVD

Matching dreams and fantasies

commentaries reveal that much of the dialogue was spontaneous, but the scene's design and its use of parallel incidents has patently been carefully determined.

Having failed to defuse their new troubling feelings for each other by pairing each with the other's *other* best friend, Harry and Sally both find another temporary partner, and the occasion at which the audience is introduced to these characters is the party at Jess and Marie's where the group plays the drawing game. Sally tries to convey the phrase 'Baby Talk' to her teammates, but they fail to guess it, and her team loses. Sally mopes about her poor drawing skills, but her new beau, Julian (Franc Luz), tells her he can see what she was trying to do. This is a kind gesture, but Harry has also tried to defend Sally in his own way, using his habitual comic banter to insult Jess. Harry and Sally each have a moment where they behold the other kiss the new partner, and both drop their eyes, Harry in disappointment, Sally, with some of Ryan's customary physical comedy, making a wry face that strives for nonchalance but actually signals her intense interest.

In another one of those satisfyingly matching scenes with which the film brims, Harry then dismisses Julian to Jess, while Sally criticises Harry's new girl Emily (Tracy Reiner) to Marie. The parallel moments show them being proprietorial about each other, claiming better knowledge of their preferences ('Sally hates baseball'/'Harry doesn't even like sweets'). Interestingly, the quality that each has condemned in the other's new partner (Julian is 'a little stuffy', Emily 'a little young') is then remarked upon by them too, with Sally acknowledging Julian is 'a grown-up', and Harry resorting to humour to show that Emily is indeed a little young, as well as clueless about politics and popular culture. While Jess and Marie delicately try to steer them away from criticism of the other's new partner with a compliment about theirs, Harry and Sally here further reveal the mutuality of their feelings through the symmetry in what they say and feel about the other's new partner – who they both clearly see as rivals.

Sex

As the narrative has been carefully manoeuvring the pair closer and closer, the viewer may experience mixed feelings when the union is finally achieved. Genre, star names, couch couple comparisons, narrative and script have all been working to bring Harry and Sally together, and when this is accomplished there is some satisfaction. However, although Sally's misery is both poignantly and comically enacted by Ryan, and the ensuing kissing and its escalation feels natural and spontaneous, as an expression of their feelings for each other, it is because they express these feelings *physically* rather than *verbally* that the situation becomes problematic the minute the sex is over. If only they had declared their love first! By the time they have finished, the status of their relationship has changed forever, and they seem to have fulfilled Harry's early assertion that men and women can't be just friends.

This leads both of them to ring their *other* best friends, and this in turn results in Harry talking to Jess as Marie is on the phone with Sally. The split-screen of the *Casablanca* sequence is both echoed and extended here: Harry on the lefthand side of the screen and Sally on the right, bracket their friends, who are sharing an actual bed, but the rupture in the central couple's relationship is visibly rendered by the

The split-screen now emphasises the distance between the central couple

distance between them, now filled in the frame with the other people to whom they turn for guidance.

It is ironic that, although they are emotionally estranged at this point, Harry and Sally still have a core connection that means their dialogue is paralleled: 'We did it', they announce together. The fluid ebb and flow of events in this whole sequence can again lead us to overlook its careful structuring: phone calls bracket the pivotal moment, the first bringing the protagonists together, the second announcing their emotional separation.

Ending

Again there are parallel moments, contrasting this initially sad New Year's to the previous one's happy if frustrating times. This final section is another that also marries sound and image via complex editing, showing the two thinking about each other as the film gradually moves towards its satisfying resolution. Scenes with Harry alternate with those devoted to Sally, linking them together in space and time to underline how much each is in the thoughts of the other.

Both are having a bad time. Harry at first is home alone with only the television for company, Sally by contrast at a crowded party, but both are equally lonely. Harry then is seen out on the streets of New York; his voiceover has him asserting that he is having fun although he obviously isn't; as he stops to stare in a shop window he hears a woman laugh. This reminds him of Sally, who has usually been obliging enough to laugh at his jokes; it is interesting that he misses her reacting to his humour: he wants a woman who will laugh at his shtik. On the soundtrack under this shot is a piano, picking out the notes of 'But Not for Me' again slowly, and again this is an appropriate track for someone feeling left out of romance.

Sally by contrast hears 'Isn't It Romantic?' playing at the party, but this proves to be inappropriate as a man is telling her a dirty joke, which Sally evidently does not find funny; though she laughs, her forlorn aside to Marie reveals her real feelings. Matched actions continue to link the pair across the space of the city – Harry hears a

Laughter links the former friends across the city's
spaces, even though both are miserable

The epiphanic montage: Harry remembers the good times with Sally

woman laugh, Sally forces a laugh – which underlines, as so often, the mutuality of their feelings.

When Harry reaches the arch of Washington Square Park, he experiences memories of Sally that are crafted into a romance-recapping montage for the viewer. It is interesting that this is very similar to one in *Annie Hall*, although here substantially reduced in length and strictly chronological. While the voices of the two friends are heard over 'But Not for Me', having the debate about whether men and women can just be friends, the sequence of images revisits the arc of their relationship in seven shots: they shake hands goodbye at the Arch; they sit together on the plane; they walk in the park smiling, just before she announces that they are going to be friends; she tells him about her sex fantasy; they laugh in the museum; she fakes the orgasm in the deli; and they begin to embrace just before their night together.

As Sally's voice finishes with her line about Harry, being 'the only person I knew in New York', he comes back to himself, turns and walks away from the Arch, half shrugging and sighing. As Frank Sinatra's vocals finally well up in his version of their song, 'It Had to Be You', Harry has his epiphany, realises he loves her and starts to run to her.

As the scene shifts back to Sally at the party, the sound of Sinatra's voice shifts with it. While before they both heard separate soundtracks, Harry's in his head, Sally's playing in the room, now his romantic realisation is enough to link them both by sound across their disparate spaces. As the narrative accelerates to bring the two together finally, the cuts between them also accelerate, with Harry running to be at the party, then Sally making ready to leave. Finally as she moves through the crowd she stops, looking surprised, and the camera permits us the sight of what has stopped her: Harry arriving.

Although Harry admits at once without banter that he loves her, Sally postpones the happy ending for which the audience is by now primed. She assumes he is just feeling lonely at New Year, but he denies this and then, comically and romantically, lists things he loves about her, including her fussy eating. We have seen Sally respond to his comedy routines before with laughter, with annoyance and with resignation, but this is the first time she attempts to comment on his shtik habit, as if the detachment this should give her will let her reject him, but as she tells him this is a typically appealing line from him, she finds herself in tears.

Harry's declaration of love, like his pass from the first diner scene, is now 'out there', but Nora Ephron refuses to let Sally match it with the obvious rejoinder. Instead Sally reiterates that she hates him, even as she cries and passionately kisses him.

This is most unusual for the big climax of a romcom and is the one moment where the neat balance of Harry and Sally's lines and experiences is avoided. Harry does not seem daunted by her declaration, though, and rightly. As they surface from their embrace and smile at each other he performs another one of his customary comic moments, joking about the unfathomable lyrics of 'Auld Lang Syne'. Sally rolls her eyes at this, but gets the last word, asserting that the song, just like the film itself, is about old friends.

As their voices then discuss the stages of their relationship, Sally and Harry appear on the couples couch, becoming the seventh and final pair to be interviewed about their meet cute. They thus dissolve, by moving from narrative segment to interlude, the carefully composed structure of the film, which has alternated these different sections and kept them separate, though related, throughout. As the film has worked to break down the barriers between them, Harry and Sally now break down the strict opposition of interlude and narrative, moving from the developing to attained couple status that the couch confers, and ending their story with the implication that they will live as happily ever after as the other testimonial couples who have preceded them.

Interlude 5 – *imitation is the sincerest form ...*

'Harry', played by Billy Crystal, sits in a diner, with half a sandwich in his hand. Opposite him is a pretty, perky blonde, and they are arguing about his ability to tell whether a woman is faking it. Harry

asserts that no woman has faked it with him before, and he could tell if she tried. His female companion smirks. She inhales. She starts to breathe heavily. She makes more and more noise, attracting more and more attention, until finally, at the climax of her performance: 'ATCHOOO!' Miss Piggy smirks as she finishes her pretend sneeze, while a patron at another table calls to a nearby waiter, 'I'll have what she's having – only less pepper.'

This parody, from *Muppets Tonight* (ABC, 1996) testifies to the lasting impact the famous 'deli scene' has had within popular culture. Although other scenes and incidents from the film are sometimes spoofed or referenced, as with the couch couple echoes mentioned in Interlude 2, it is the deli scene that has generated the most extensive wave of copies. Why should the concept of faking an orgasm in a public place be so profoundly influential?

If we consider the *Muppets* parody in detail we can perhaps find out. In the sketch, Crystal reprises his wiseguy persona, refusing to believe any woman would fake a sneeze with him, and then repeats his largely reaction-bound routine from the film as Miss Piggy delivers her over-the-top performance.

The sketch is funny because of the drastic nature of the build-up to the sneeze, the force of which makes Miss Piggy career around the restaurant and finally blows Harry and his chair away from the table, ensuring that it is equally amusing to children or anyone not in on the

'Harry' is dismissive; 'Sally' fakes it (*Muppets Tonight*, 1996)

movie allusion. Where the parody taps into the original, however, is not only in its re-enactment of the faked orgasm as a sneeze. It also borrows snippets of dialogue, such as 'on the side' and 'hot date'. It puts Harry into a similar chunky sweater, and he addresses his companion explicitly as 'Sally'. Perhaps the neatest touch is the add-on 'with less pepper', to the scene's concluding line, which harks back to Crystal's funny-accented improv about 'paprikash' in the Temple of Dendur scene.

The scriptwriters knew the movie well, then, but why spoof it? Perhaps because there is something irresistible in seeing a wiseguy get his comeuppance. The *Muppets* sequence makes sure to include Crystal's moment of arrogant self-assurance – 'You don't think that I could tell the difference? Get outta here!' – so that Miss Piggy gets to prove him wrong, punishing him for his ignorance and conceit, just as Sally does in the original.

Of the many spoofs of the deli scene, the *Muppets Tonight* parody stands out for this reason: it does more than simply recycle the loud acclamation, public eating space, mortified vis-à-vis. The PG Tips Monkey, in 2010, prompted to describe the taste of the tea, goes into the by-now familiar routine, pounding the table and yodelling 'Splendid!' But his reaction is supposed to be sincere. The joke gets lost if the over-excited person is actually truly enjoying the sensation.

Similarly, a reprisal of the scene in *The Ugly Truth* (2009) clearly shows just why critics are always pronouncing the romantic comedy dead. The newer scene unfolds as if it were in homage to *When Harry Met Sally...* but vital aspects differ. Some of the expected elements remain: a crowded eaterie, a woman's vocal performance of sexual excitement, bewilderment from her fellow diners. What is missing, crucially, is the character's *agency*: Abby (Katherine Heigl) *just happens* to be wearing vibrating panties and *just happens* to take their remote control out with her to an important business dinner and then *just happens* to lose the remote, which is operated, in ignorance, by a pre-teenage boy. Heigl's performance of her character's real orgasm is comic, just as Ryan's of Sally's fake one

was twenty years before, but it is made so much less enjoyable because she is not faking the sensations to teach a man a lesson, but having them genuinely evoked within her body, without her permission or even the knowledge of who is doing it.

Narrative Segment 5 – *reception*

When Harry Met Sally... was released on 14 July 1989 and instantly attracted much critical attention. While the film enjoys a generally positive reputation now, at the time the response was very much divided and, although an ad in *Daily Variety* after the opening weekend claimed 'EVERYONE LOVES "WHEN HARRY MET SALLY...",[35] this was plainly not the case.

One factor behind its popularity was that it was atypical of film fare at the time, in this 'Summer of the Sequel',[36] when the romantic comedy was under-represented at the box office.

Several critics believed these were reasons to celebrate its release. *Rolling Stone* began with the cry 'Attention, sequel sufferers',[37] announcing 'welcome relief' to blockbuster-jaded audiences. *TIME* agreed, calling it and the also recently released *sex, lies and videotape* 'two comedies that waft like zephyrs through a movie summer humid with macho derring-do'.[38] The *Los Angeles Times* highlighted its status as an original story in two separate responses, first in its official review quoted above, and then two weeks later: 'The literate adult romantic comedy is not dead, only

A putative homage to *When Harry Met Sally...* (Katherine Heigl and Gerard Butler in *The Ugly Truth*, 2009)

scarce now as always. And when one comes along, it is an occasion for glad cries of joy and full houses.'[39]

When Harry Met Sally... was hailed as a welcome change from the summer slate of superhero, special-effects and action movies, and from the – often overlapping – slew of sequels. Between May and July 1989, the movie theatres of America were saturated with such fare. Offering an intimate story about personal relationships was rare at this point in the release calendar, then, but the film was also praised for being not only a romcom, but an insightful one

The campus paper of the University of California, the *UCLA Summer Bruin*, lauded it as 'the first movie in a long time to capture the nuances, contradictions and just plain hard work involved in falling in love'.[40] This recognises the core of realism in *When Harry Met Sally...* that was missing in other recent films in the genre, few as they were. Another quotation, from the *Washington Post*, takes up this point, celebrating Sally in particular: 'Neither naïf nor vamp, she's a woman from the pen of a woman, not some Cinderella of a "Working Girl"'.[41] This reference to the Mike Nichols film, released the previous December, hints that some found the earlier movie and its characters more of a masculine fantasy than the Reiner–Ephron film.

Other reviews too registered that the film persuasively exposed current social and sexual mores, while also managing to evoke traditional romantic comedies. *The Hollywood Reporter*'s ecstatic commentary on what it called a 'beautiful, brainy, touching and lifting romantic comedy' noted that it was both a 'wonderfully topical, yet wisely old-fashioned romancer'.[42] Similarly, the *LA Times* felt that it was 'linking the spirit of the great romantic comedies of Hollywood's past with the textures and realities of life in a later and less romantic time'.[43] The *LA Times* admired the film's seemingly paradoxical mixture of generic traditions and contemporary milieu, when asserting Crystal and Ryan were 'working precisely the same turf as the glorious [screwball] duos of the past', and then praising the movie's accurate capture of the zeitgeist, presenting 'a recognizable yuppie world, real to the last Reebok'.[44]

There was praise for the cinematography ('glowingly romantic',[45] 'rapturously shot'),[46] the direction ('diffidently delightful and delicately delirious'),[47] the 'starmaking performances'[48] and witty script, especially the clever dialogue ('glorious, near-seamless … often manages to be comic and revealing in the same moment').[49] With an opening line that seems to compliment Ephron by echoing Jess's sound bites on restaurants and pesto – 'Talk is the sex of the '80s' – *TIME* lauds the writer for embedding the film within the contemporary singles scene, observing that she 'perks the script with clever answers to modern problems'.[50]

Curiously, although many reviewers praised the screenplay in particular, and it featured in the marketing,[51] others denigrated it. Indeed, many of the aspects that found favour in the positive reviews were decried by the film's disparagers.

While, then, one or two of the negative commentators did allow that Ephron's dialogue was enjoyably 'sporty',[52] 'often sparkling'[53] or 'witty, epigrammatic',[54] others felt that the script was superficial, with sitcom-level insights, Ephron was 'the mistress of glib'[55] or, worse, *cuddly*:

Can a man be friends with a woman he finds attractive? Can usually acerbic scripter Nora Ephron sustain 95 minutes of unrelenting cuteness? Can the audience sit through 11 years of emotional foreplay between adorable Billy Crystal and Meg Ryan?[56]

One predominantly adverse reaction, from *The Village Voice*, adroitly located the central voice in the film as Ephron's, even though, as she and Reiner acknowledge, its incidents were frequently drawn from his dating experiences. The review noted the film 'works by reprises, choral refrains', or by individual 'tics, often to do with eating'.[57] Although this review concluded that Ephron's trick of individualising people through traits was shallow, it is significant that her methods of building characters and structuring the narrative were perceived, if not appreciated. *Screen International* by contrast refuted the writer's skill, condemning 'the usual formulaic pastiche of scenes of the couple taking walks, shopping and dining together'.[58] Since such scenes convey the development of the relationship, it is mistaken to view them as 'pastiche', as they are central to Ephron's conception of the contemporary backdrops to romance.

It is fascinating to see just how much the film originally divided critics: of twenty-six reviews from major newspapers, trade journals and literary magazines, sixteen were negative, with one opinion almost ubiquitous. Critics often felt that the movie was too clichéd; while those who enjoyed it could appreciate its handling of traditional romcom tropes, those who disliked it, including *People* magazine[59] and *Newsweek*, felt this same practice revealed the film-makers' lack of imagination. The *New Republic*'s bald assertion, 'The plot is highly unoriginal',[60] seemed to sum up the view of many periodicals' critics.

Another common condemnation was that the film was unrealistic. This frequent criticism does not seem to be cross-referenced against genre expectations to explain why the film would spend more time on the characters' love lives than developing their work environments. Several of the adversarial critics dismissed the film for having characters that seemed to live in a love bubble: 'no one ever talks about work or career or books or politics or family', kvetched the *LA Herald-Examiner*.[61] 'Work in this movie has been relegated to "another sphere"', agreed *The Village Voice*.[62] And *LA Weekly* was similarly irate: 'none of these people spend much time talking about their work – the epitome of self-definition for New Yorkers'.[63]

While these commentators seem to want to nudge the film away from its romcom status, others dismissed it as unrealistic but managed to accept choices based on generic allegiance, and attacked the characterisation instead. The deli scene was frequently cited here. Even while some found the incident funny, these critics felt uptight

Sally Albright was departing from character in making a spectacle of herself, as *The New Yorker* complained:

... to find the scene uproarious you have to forget everything the picture has told us about the character. She's neat, controlled, a bit of a goody-goody, so what little personality she has been given is violated by this unembarrassed public performance.[64]

The *Village View* critic agreed that this display was 'totally at odds' with Sally's personality and felt the director had sacrificed character consistency here: 'Funny, yes. Good filmmaking, no.'[65] It seems so ironic that one of the film's most celebrated and cherished moments should have been singled out for negative commentary.

Interlude 6 – *running*

I want here to investigate one trope condemned in some negative reviews that has subsequently become quite commonplace in romantic comedies:

About the ending I shall only say this: It is a serious mistake to show Crystal doing something beginning with R (a three-letter word ending in N) that at least two other short New York actors (W.A. and D.H) have done enough of already.[66]

Harry's run to get to Sally at the end was here amusingly condemned by the *Village Voice* critic; by mentioning Crystal's height, she shows she is reminded of Dustin Hoffman's run through the streets of Manhattan in family drama *Kramer vs. Kramer* (1979) – or possibly the thriller, *Marathon Man* (1976) – and is therefore prepared to ignore genre specificity to make a height joke. Other reviews which noted Harry's headlong rush to reclaim Sally felt the run was either stolen from Allen,[67] or direct from the genre handbook, since *The New Republic* described this trope as the 'most worn of all'[68] romantic comedy conventions.

The running trope in romantic comedies seems to enjoy contemporary popularity, making an appearance in *Sleepless in Seattle* (1993), *Only You* (1994), *Not Another Teen Movie* (2001), *Love Actually* (2003), *Imagine Me and You* (2005), *Starter for Ten* (2006), *Life as We Know It* (2010), *L'Arnacoeur/Heartbreakers* (2010), *She's out of My League* (2010) and in *El Critico/The Critic* (2013), *Playing It Cool* and *They Came Together* (both 2014), and *Sleeping with Other People* (2015) is used explicitly self-consciously.

While it might then appear quite a new convention, it actually pre-dates sound cinema. Harold Lloyd's character runs to stop the wedding of his beloved (Jobyna Ralston) in 1924's *Girl Shy*; over the

The running scene... in *Kramer vs. Kramer* (1979); ... in the romcom within a romcom, in *Friends with Benefits* (2011) ...

course of an exhilarating twenty-minute sequence, in his rush to reach her he appropriates various vehicles which each comically fail. The film maintains suspense by having his headlong approach cut against the crawlingly slow progress of the reluctant bride, but eventually she says 'I do'. No matter: Harold bursts in just before the minister can pronounce them man and wife. Throwing her over his shoulder, he departs with the woman as fast as he arrived, carrying her away to safety where he proves the groom was already married.

The bride's passivity here is played for comic effect in this film; a more assertive one is played by Claudette Colbert in *It Happened One Night* (1934). She too gets down the aisle and to the moment of saying her vows when she realises she loves another, Peter Warne (Clark Gable), and sprints away from her own ceremony, her long train streaming out behind her as she dashes across the lawn.

These two film moments illustrate two of the earliest examples of classic archetypes within the romcom genre, the rescuing lover and the runaway bride. These figures provide the impetus for the running trope at a time when female virginity was, at least publicly, held to be extremely important. It is the irreplaceable quality of the bride's virginity that motivates the lover's dash and the wedding's interruption: once she has had her

... in *The Graduate* (1967) ...

'wedding night' with the groom, no matter how wrong he is for her, her value will be diminished.

Obviously popular cultural attachment to virginity had moderated by the time *The Graduate* made use of the same trope in 1967; not only has Benjamin Braddock (Dustin Hoffman) slept with the bride already, he has also slept with her mother. This is perhaps why the film allows him – after *another* protracted Hoffman running scene – to get to the church too late to stop the vows being exchanged; his lateness also permits the still more shocking abandonment of her lawful husband by Elaine (Katharine Ross) as she and Benjamin run away and escape by bus to their uncertain future.

... in *When Harry Met Sally...*; and in *Manhattan* (1979)

In more recent romantic comedies, it has become the fashion to have one of the lovers rush to stop the other leaving the country, so the airport has become the locus of the run, but city streets serve just as well. Although the *Village Voice* critic felt Harry's run was too like Isaac's in *Manhattan*, and whichever Hoffman film she was remembering, I think Ephron provides her hero with a better motive for his hurry, in that he wants to be with Sally as soon as possible once he realises she is the one. Tracy (Mariel Hemingway), Isaac's ex-girlfriend, whose imminent departure for the airport and then London motivated his dash, rebukes him gently when she reminds him 'I'll be back in six months'. One of the reasons the running convention often feels forced is because screenwriters are endowing the departure with the same irreparable quality that virginity once held, but people can talk on the phone, or email or be visited. It is much more romantic that Harry runs because he just does not want to waste any more of his life without Sally.

Narrative Segment 6 – 'Woody lite'[69]

By far the most common observation, from both pro and con reviewers of the film, was the resemblance of *When Harry Met Sally...* to movies directed by Woody Allen. The *New York Times* review dismissed the Ephron–Reiner movie as being like 'the sitcom version of a Woody Allen film', ending by denouncing it as a 'Woody Allen wannabe';[70] the similarity of the later film to Allen's was also criticised by *LA Weekly*, which regretted there was 'no muscle tone under the hommage'.[71] *7 Days*, although more well disposed to the film, which it praised as 'the one laugh-out-loud comedy of the summer that won't leave you feeling embarrassed afterward', still concluded that 'the spirit of the Woodman hovers over this movie [...] inescapably'.[72]

Overall, reviews seemed to insist that Allen handled the shared themes and locales better, bristling that any other film-makers would even dare to take these on. *The Village Voice* drily noted that while 'Woody Allen has taken a lot of flak for his romantic New York', the newer film was even more artificial: 'nothing in Allen looks as saccharine as [...] these locations'.[73] The most definitive put-down came from *The Orange County Register*, which damned it as 'not altogether bad, just unnecessary'.[74]

In all, fourteen of the negative reviews, as well as seven of the positive – that is, twenty-one out of the twenty-six consulted – felt that Ephron and Reiner were trying to 'muscle in on Woody Allen territory'.[75] Although the adverse critics were united in expressing their dislike for other film-makers taking on topics and tropes they felt belonged to Allen, it is interesting to note *who* is blamed for the appropriation. The *Orlando Sentinel* review dismissed director Reiner as insignificant, faulting the writer instead:

I would never have thought Ephron capable of something as blatantly imitative as *When Harry Met Sally...*

After watching the film, I've drastically revised my opinion of Nora Ephron. If I were to hear that she's now appearing in Vegas as an Elvis impersonator, I would not be a bit surprised.[76]

More often, the director was held to blame for the theft, as we can see in repeated article titles; 'When Rob Met Woody' was used for both the *Chicago Tribune* and the *LA Weekly* reviews, while *The Orange County Register* enlarged only a little with 'Harry meets Sally, Rob meets Woody'. Perhaps the auteur status of Allen impelled critics to attack, specifically, any other *director* who seemed to borrow from him:

The opening credits feature Woody Allen's trademark white letters on a black background with a jaunty version of 'It Had to Be You' on the soundtrack. The score is rich with Gershwin, the camera infatuated with Manhattan, the dialogue obsessed with sex, love and death. Altogether, 'When Harry Met Sally...' is the most blatant bow from one director to another since Mr Allen imitated Ingmar Bergman in 'Interiors'.[77]

I think something in all this criticism smacks of intellectual snobbery. When Allen borrows from Bergman, he is consciously making an *hommage* to a master of European cinema – just recognising that fact grants the viewer cachet. But potential borrowing from the American director is viewed as theft, and I can only conclude it is because a fun movie has dared to emulate aspects of others considered to have more cultural capital.

One word used in both the attacks quoted above seems significant here: 'blatant'. Perhaps it is the transparency of this recycling that annoyed reviewers. Those who felt so strongly that *When Harry Met Sally...* had purloined features from Allen were basing their judgment on two separate, debatable, points. They assumed first that Allen had used various elements in his films so often that they had become his signature, and second that the later film consciously stole this personal property. Features that they pointed to as co-opted in this way included the:

- black and white credits
- musical score relying on classic songs from the popular jazz songbook
- direct-to-camera interviews
- Manhattan locations
- costume
- cinephilia – the love of old movies, especially *Casablanca*.

Earlier sections have considered the origins of the couch couple/ witness segments, and the music, so what I want to look at here are two other elements condemned as thefts: New York City and *Casablanca*.

Ten periodicals[78] seemed to imply that simply setting a romcom in New York meant Ephron and Reiner were guilty of copying Allen. Criticism was sometimes general and sometimes specific about which particular Allen films were being imitated. *Variety* went for the first approach, insisting 'the film conjures up an image of Manhattan that recalls Woody Allen's cinematic love affair with the city';[79] *The New*

York Times, by contrast, indulged in a more detailed dissection: 'Harry and Sally's version of the city offers constant jolts of recognition, as it dwells on carefully specified landmarks and echoes *Annie Hall* and *Manhattan*.'[80]

Although more recently it has been common to use New York City as the locus of love, the place where romance inevitably happens,[81] and contemporary romantic comedies offer up the same glimpses of the city time and again, providing a clichéd tourist view of Manhattan, the meaning of the location in the early 1970s, against which Allen and others rebelled, was very different. Gritty police dramas and Blaxploitation movies such as *The French Connection* (1971) and *Super Fly* (1972) had used the city's real-life dirt and crime to underline the danger of the metropolis: at that point in popular culture it represented much more *Mean Streets* (1973) than *Breakfast at Tiffany's* (1961).

This was the very reason that those behind what I have elsewhere called 'the radical romcom'[82] chose to situate their love stories in New York: if romance could exist for a couple there, in the ultimate symbol of urban alienation, there was a chance for the rest of us. While *Annie Hall* was one of these radical romcoms it was by no means the only example: Paul Mazursky's *An Unmarried Woman* (1978) made much of the city's swift tempo, grime and pollution, and lonely, frustrated inhabitants the year after *Annie Hall*, but *The Goodbye Girl*, directed by Herbert Ross from a Neil Simon script, contained the same elements the same year, 1977, appearing in movie theatres over a month before the Allen film.

Although these films contributed to the mid-70s rehabilitation of New York City from its image as a centre of crime and loneliness, the city had been portrayed as the locale of excitement and glamour, *the* place for the fulfilment of romantic and erotic desires, actually since the beginnings of cinema, but notably in films from the late 1920s onwards, such as *The Love Trap* (1929), *Girls about Town* (1931) and *Careless Lady* (1932). The career-girl comedies of the mid- to late 1950s, which pit small-town girls against big-city

Romeos, such as *Ask Any Girl* and *Pillow Talk* (both 1959) also plainly exploited this strand of the city's reputation. The 70s romcoms set in Manhattan were therefore *returning* romance to the city rather than introducing it.

The Manhattan setting might also represent an instance of cinephilia. *When Harry Met Sally...* is a movie-savvy movie; not only do the characters talk about favourite films, but the text also nods to other pictures besides Woody Allen's. Viewed as part of the film-makers' shared love letter not just to New York, but also to cinema itself, the decision to situate its narrative in specific recognisable sites could be defended as a conscious attempt to invoke other New York-set film texts, such as *Pillow Talk*. Nora Ephron would prove how acutely aware she was of the city's cinematic heritage when compiling the tribute for the 50th Academy Awards in 2002, the year after the September 2001 terrorist attacks. Ephron's montage pays homage not only to Allen but also to Martin Scorsese and many other directors who have taken the city as inspiration.[83]

Whether the film's representation of cinephilia, its characters' and its makers' love of film, is enough to justify the inclusion of a reference to *Casablanca* is an interesting question. Many of the negative reviewers felt it was not, but that any reference to the 1942 film inevitably evoked not its own director, Michael Curtiz, but Allen. He had co-opted *Casablanca* for the plot of his play (1969) and then film (1972), *Play It Again, Sam*, in which the lead character believes himself advised in romantic matters by the spirit of Bogart.

For *The Orange County Register*, one of the most negatively inclined of the daily papers, the *Casablanca* reference was just too much:

... even the main characters' affection for 'Casablanca' becomes suspect. Admittedly, a lot of people love 'Casablanca'. But in a context that is continuously conjuring memories of Woody Allen, a scene in which Harry and Sally watch the famous airport ending feels like yet another crib from Allen, echoing the central obsession in 'Play It Again, Sam'. Conspiracy or coincidence? You decide.[84]

This reviewer obviously inclines to the conspiracy theory, not being persuaded that Ephron's inclusion of *Casablanca* is motivated by the wish to tie that film's famous last lines about friendship into her own narrative on this topic. It should be acknowledged, however, that other films are referenced, both overtly and in a more subterranean fashion. When Sally and Marie are in 'Shakespeare and Co' and see Harry, Marie invokes Alfred Hitchcock's 1938 comedy-thriller, *The Lady Vanishes*, to suggest her friend's initial dislike of the man might end similarly romantically. Harry gleefully sings a song from the musical, *Oklahoma!*[85] and later, when morosely window-shopping on New Year's Eve, stares at a number of miniature heads of characters from *The Wizard Of Oz* (1939) – Dorothy, The Wicked Witch, The Scarecrow – and Laurel and Hardy. The film thus openly situates its own story in the context of other filmic narratives by reflecting the contemporary popular culture in which its characters live, a popular culture which celebrates classic films, stars, characters and moments.

Ephron and Reiner's awareness of past film stories and techniques also extends to the incorporation of more veiled references and borrowings, as with the aforementioned split-screen scenes (like *Indiscreet* and *Pillow Talk*), and in the covert nod to film noir classic *Gilda* (1946) at the climax of their film. Gilda (Rita Hayworth) and her gangster-husband's henchman Johnny (Glenn Ford) are former lovers; when he re-encounters her as his boss's wife he is furious. Gilda purrs seductively in response to his angry admission that he hates her: 'Hate is a very exciting emotion [...] I hate you too, Johnny. I hate you so much I think I'm going to die from it ... *darling*!' – and they kiss. In having Sally refuse to provide the usual answer to Harry's declaration of love, Ephron subtly evokes the older film's lines to indicate the depth of Sally's feelings, even as she also marks herself out as a cinephile screenwriter aware of romcom conventions and prepared to subvert them.

The familiarity of themes and tropes was commented on in some positive reviews also, but generally these seemed much more

nonchalant about its film-makers treading the same path as Allen.
The *LA Times* contended that '"Harry/Sally" has an irrepressible,
crackling rhythm that is Reiner's own. And is it necessarily bad if a
film shares Allen's territory and even some of his attitudes?
Sheesh!'[86] *Rolling Stone* agreed about the similarities: 'So what?
Woody, now stuck in a turgid mode, has long since abandoned
Annie Hall territory.'[87] This latter comment implies that, if an
appetite remains for talky New York romcoms, now Allen has
ceased to make them, they are fair game for others. While both these
reviews affirm approval of *When Harry Met Sally...*, they also
assume its status as Allen copy and the romantic comedy genre as his
property. The principal of the film's production company, Castle
Rock, Martin Shafer, however, contested this in an interview in trade
paper *The Hollywood Reporter*:

because a movie has a certain amount of intelligence and humor and the
people are actually talking to each other, it's automatically compared to a
Woody Allen movie. Can no one else make a movie with intelligence and
humor? Is that forbidden ground or something?[88]

Shafer makes a valid point. And at this distance, nearly thirty years
after the film's release, the controversy over whether *When Harry
Met Sally...* was just too much of a 'Woody Allen wannabe',
consciously or not, seems less important. Nonetheless, is it possible to
give a definitive answer to the 'conspiracy or coincidence' question
posed by *The Orange County Register*? My take on the matter would
be this: the echoes of Allen in the later film could be viewed as
coincidences. As Shafer indicated, being intelligent and wordy did not
mean a film was necessarily imitating Woody Allen.

Other alternatives remain, however. One would be to see the
coincidence of elements as a conscious decision, but with the film-
makers considering New York or *Casablanca* generic conventions
now available to anyone. Ephron, in particular, was evidently aware
of the genre's devices and was prepared to avoid or mock them; her

refusal to let Sally answer 'I love you too' at the film's conclusion, and her subversion of the 'meet cute' formula, indicate her ability to confound expectation. Furthermore, whatever the critics say, Ephron was working in a talky mode that is not 'Allenesque', but harked back to an older style of comedy that, bound by Production Code conventions about what could be shown on screen, needed to derive its charge from witty, allusive and frequently adversarial dialogue between the female and male protagonists.

A further suggestion is that the 1989 film was intended as an homage to Allen. Any similarities therefore could be seen in the spirit of playful in-jokes, not trying to get one over on audiences and critics. The problem with this suggestion is that we might expect an acknowledgment of this intention by Reiner or Ephron, and there is none; even in their discussion on the 2008 DVD, a perfect opportunity for a post hoc confession, the pair only comment that Allen had made it difficult to find anywhere in Manhattan he had not already shot – which would rather imply a conscious wish to *avoid* copying him.

The final possibility is that the conscious copy was made with a twist – it was not intended to be flattering but barbed. This would imply the film-makers had set out to use elements of Allen films schematically but not in praise of their originals or their maker. This kind of combative copying would be less likely to be acknowledged in a DVD commentary. While I think it entirely possible to watch and enjoy the film without worrying about any of these potential solutions, this latter is given support by various elements throughout the text. For example, at the start of the film, a surtitle confirms the year as 1977: while this may be just historicising information, like Sally's period-appropriate 'Farrah flip' hair-do, it is also the year of *Annie Hall*'s release. A further detail is the 'dippy bird' Harry stares at in the montage where we see him grieving after his break-up with Helen. This might just be a random item in Harry's office, but there is a giant dippy bird used as a decorative feature in Luna's (Diane Keaton) house in Allen's *Sleeper* (1973); so this could be an inane

'executive toy', but it could also be taken as a reference to the Allen film by those in on the joke.

My suggestion would be that Harry Burns does not just represent the archetypal Allenesque *hero*, although he does have the 'proud to be miserabilist' shtik going on, but rather Allen's entire *brand* of 'nervous romance'. In this formulation, the film-makers would have revealed the innate masculine bias of his romantic

Harry's dippy bird; the giant dippy bird, in *Sleeper* (1973)

comedies by using elements of Allen's films; the use of the jazz standards familiar from Allen films, for example, would thus be significant, acting as the soundtrack to the hero's self-indulgent narcissism rather than the romance. Correcting the Allen model, the Ephron–Reiner film could be seen as achieving a more equable division of power between the lovers, by inventing a more well-rounded heroine, and in this way opposing her to the 70s Allen woman, like Annie or Tracy from *Manhattan*, who is never properly knowable, never more desired than when pushed away.

While it is impossible to assert definitively which, if any, of these options is the true one, I like the last idea: that Ephron and Reiner consciously embarked into 'Woody Allen territory' as a corrective to his unequal romances.

Narrative Segment 7 – *legacy*

When Harry Met Sally... is so much more than a faked orgasm and a punchline. Not only does it offer many more pleasures than these, admittedly fine comic moments, it also stands as a pivotal film that helped reinvigorate the romantic comedy genre. Paradoxically, the film is well loved but also misunderstood and underappreciated: viewers know it is good, funny and poignant, but perhaps do not fully realise how important and influential it is. But *When Harry Met Sally...* is worthy of a place in a romcom pantheon with other films that introduced or perfected a whole new subgenre, like *It Happened One Night* (1934) with the screwball, *Pillow Talk* with the battle-of-the-sexes comedy and *Annie Hall* with the radical romcom; *When Harry Met Sally...* is similarly transformative.

It needs to be appreciated as a pivotal film in two ways: for stimulating a revival of the romantic comedy after the genre had idled for over a decade, and for reinvigorating the products of that genre in ways that changed what romcom meant and could do.

As mentioned earlier, it was released in a decade in which the romcom was extremely under-represented at the box office. In looking at the increased number of romantic comedies that began to appear after *When Harry Met Sally...* I am not arguing that these later films were made expressly because of its success, but rather that its popularity indicated audience hunger for such films, and that other directors then began to tap into this with more confidence. Indeed, year on year across the succeeding decade the romcom came back into its own, increasing from 1990's two romcom hits to five in 1993, eight in 1995, ten in 1997 and so on to a high of thirteen in 1999. *When Harry Met Sally...* had indicated that the romcom could be big business again and, while hardly any of the films that followed could match its combination of traditional conventions and innovative elements, many obviously tried to emulate its success by borrowing directly from it.

It may seem strange that a film as popular as *When Harry Met Sally...* now is needs to be dissected to reveal what it does so audaciously and brilliantly, but in order to understand it for the trailblazer it was, I think analysis is necessary. It must be obvious by now how much I admire the film's structure, which provides a scaffolding that is subtle yet secure and satisfying, with beats, suspense, symmetry and returns built in. In homage to the seven narrative segments and seven interludes, I'd like to suggest another seven: seven ways in which the film was exciting and pioneering at the time – and now.

First, it introduced its central couple and then dropped them for five years – and then did it again. When other romcoms make narrative fodder out of the events of *One Fine Day* (1996) or one night (*Nick and Norah's Infinite Playlist*, 2008), one of the Reiner–Ephron film's most audacious moves is to stretch its story out over twelve years. Richard Linklater might perhaps be seen as responding to this in allowing a real-time gap of nine years to elapse between filming *Before Sunrise* (1995), its original companion piece, *Before Sunset* (2004) and its most recent return, *Before Midnight* (2013).

Second, then, *When Harry Met Sally...* gave realism back to the genre, which is one reason it is so well loved. The protagonists do not meet cute, fall in love at first sight, know instantly they have met The

One and then spend forever loving that person. Like people in real life, they get it wrong, get hurt, get older, get closer, get it wrong again, then finally learn how and when to make amends, and get married. This is a much more credible timeline, which lets us relate to the protagonists and their narrative. And then when they do get together, there is no dramatic *deus ex machina*, no great reversal of fortune, no car crash or coma, to make them realise, just their separation and then a growing realisation of what they mean to each other. The evident regret that bedevils Harry towards the finale is very realistic, even if he remains largely in denial of it.

Third, as continually mentioned, the film is beautifully structured, but so lightly that it is perfectly possible just to enjoy the parallels, echoes and returns without closer analysis. And this leads to fourth, which is the movie's enjoyably complex editing and sound mixes, and its recourse to a range of filmic techniques, such as split-screen, voiceover and montage, which both enrich the film itself *and* gesture in affectionate tribute to some of the great romantic comedies of the past.

Fifth, *When Harry Met Sally...* is funny, with not only a great written script but inspired improvisation from a quartet and more of actors who give excellent performances. And again, leading on from this, is sixth: its heroine. This is a film in which the heroine is not a cipher, not a fantasy of a woman (unlike *Working Girl's* sexy Cinderella who has 'a head for business and a bod for sin') but a character as well rounded as the man she spars with and learns to love. As much popular culture debate about Bechdel Tests[89] and Manic Pixie Dream Girls[90] has shown lately, the concept of the fully rounded female lead character is sadly all too uncommon now.

Seventh and finally, the film has been influential, not only in establishing that the romcom could be profitable at the box office, but that the genre, although one of the very oldest in cinema, could continue to evolve and renew itself.

Video website 'Funny or Die'[91] made a follow-up to the film in 2011, written by Crystal's sons-in law and directed by one of his daughters, which actively involved Reiner and Crystal, and was an imagining of the Harry character in old age, after Sally's death. While this does not sound particularly promising for a comedy short, the sequel introduced a new love interest in the form of Sharon (Helen Mirren), who confirmed her rightness for Harry by ordering dinner in the familiar, high-maintenance way. Overall, however, more comedy is directed towards contemporary Hollywood and its current impetus towards horror franchises than to the original film: the studio boss green-lighting their sequel says he has a few suggestions – which involve turning the new old lovers into 'grampires'. The woman given the Estelle Reiner line is then pounced on before she can complete the famous saying.

While the idea of the movie, which becomes *When Sharon Bit Harry*,[92] lightly mocked Hollywood's love of vampire and zombie fare, the spoof contains a kernel of truth in that the standard romcom was then becoming more difficult to get made. In a somewhat reductive argument, media websites and Hollywood trade organs such as *The Hollywood Reporter* were quick to pronounce the genre defunct.[93] The logic seemed to be that romcoms were dying because no one wanted to see them, because the ones that *were* made were bad, because no one wanted… . This is a convoluted notion not backed up by any evidence of audience intention. What is apparent is that *When Harry Met Sally...* is frequently used as the foremost example of a successful film in the genre. Ironically in condemning the genre, the *Hollywood Reporter* piece quotes one studio executive pronouncing that 'the meet cute is dead',[94] little realising it seems that the very success of the Reiner–Ephron film was due to its ability to subvert traditional conventions like this.

I believe, however, that the romcom does endure; *The L Magazine* recently suggested that the genre has moved from big studios to independent low-budget makers[95] and to the small screen. Certainly television shows like *The Mindy Project* (2012–) continue to work over familiar territory, but its cancellation[96] may indicate that overt citation and imitation might not be as rewarding as

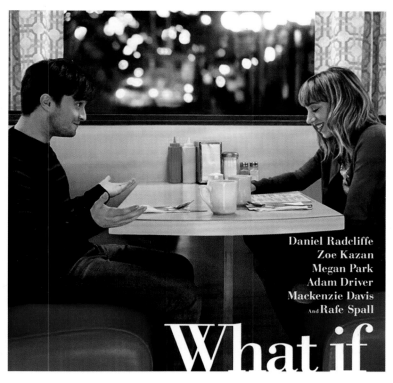

Daniel Radcliffe
Zoe Kazan
Megan Park
Adam Driver
Mackenzie Davis
And Rafe Spall

What if

...being friends has its benefits?

attempting to emulate Ephron's ambitions to make the romcom fresh, new and funny again.

Whether from conglomerate producers or tiny ones, on the big or small screen, the last few years seem to have seen a romcom revival. *What If* (2013), starring Daniel Radcliffe as a young man who agrees to be just friends with the girl he loves, obviously owed more than a superficial debt to *When Harry Met Sally...* as was evidenced by its main US poster, featuring the pair in a diner setting. Yvonne Roberts's piece on the film for the *Guardian*

The influence of *When Harry Met Sally...* remains fresh (Daniel Radcliffe and Zoe Kazan in *What If*, 2013) coupled the obvious allusion to Radcliffe's film history with the Reiner–Ephron film: 'What If "Harry Potter Meets Sally" Finally Rekindles Our Passion for the Rom-com?'[97] Roberts clearly posits the new film as both inheriting elements of the 1989 classic and possessing the potential to make viewers fall in love with the genre once more. Despite the gloom in the industry papers about the romcom's moribund status, products from the genre do continue to be made, with 2014 alone giving us both big studio and indie products: *Sex Tape, Playing It Cool, Two Night Stand, Say When, About Last Night, Cuban Fury, The Other Woman* and *Life Partners*. Another slew of romantic comedies arrived in 2015, including *The DUFF, The Wedding Ringer, Accidental Love* and *Trainwreck*. In addition, *Man Up, Tumbledown* and *Sleeping with Other People* have done well in festivals in 2015, with the latter openly taking *When Harry Met Sally...* as its model. Mentioning these three, a review on website Arts.Mic reveals its writer feels similarly optimistic about the genre, noting that for all the pronouncements of the romcom's demise, 2015 might be another watershed year: 'Rom-coms Are Back in 2015 – and They're Better Than Ever'.[98]

We only have to look at *When Harry Met Sally...* itself to see that the comic love story could come back to storm the box office if the right movie comes along. Reminding us that its genre endures might then prove to be the ultimate way in which this witty, inventive and satisfying film continues to be inspiring.

Interlude 7 – how to make two lovers of friends ...

One of the most trailblazing elements in *When Harry Met Sally...* which has since proved to be very influential in the contemporary romantic comedy, is the idea that someone's best bet for a partner is her or his best friend. The friends-and-lovers device brings together companions who have had romantic alternatives and who eventually reject those alternatives for each other. Where the formula is observable, the best friends need to be the best erotic options as well as platonic ones, but this should be overlooked by one or both until the truth is realised.

Although Ephron consciously borrowed and repurposed many elements from traditional romcoms, such as the meet cute, her screenplay largely departed from tradition in setting up the relationship between its two principals. In screwball comedy, the heroine and hero meet, sometimes fight, then realise their love; in the battle-of-the-sexes comedy, they hate each other before realising that the frisson of excitement that antagonism generates is actually a sign of love. *When Harry Met Sally...* introduced a third option, in which the woman and man are first grudging acquaintances, then friends, then lovers and then forced to confront the necessity of finding a way to be both or lose everything. This was very novel at the time and has subsequently added a scenario to the romcom playbook.

It should be noted that while Ephron and Reiner's film *popularised*, it did not entirely invent the eventually-passionate-friends motif; some films, such as 1931's *Platinum Blonde*, had played with this concept before. In this film, two dedicated newspaper reporters Stew (Robert Williams) and Gallagher (Loretta Young) are best friends, but their relationship becomes rocky when Stew marries the Platinum Blonde of the title, heiress Anne Schuyler (Jean Harlow). She dislikes his profession, however, and wants him to do something more genteel; the marriage eventually ends and he realises he has loved Gallagher all along.

Platinum Blonde provides another standard ingredient of the romantic comedy genre that Steve Neale recognises as the 'wrong partner'.[99] Neale defines the wrong partner as someone whom the central character must eventually reject, as he or she usually represents not only a disastrous romantic alternative but also some personal quality in the central character that needs to be eliminated. In *Platinum Blonde*, Anne is the wrong partner for Stew because she undermines his independence and autonomy; he has to reject his attraction to her along with his own desire for easy wealth.

Julian and Emily are the latest in a long list of wrong partners for both our protagonists, which includes Amanda and Helen for Harry and Joe (Steven Ford) for Sally. Where the Reiner–Ephron film brilliantly exceeds the wrong-partner format, however, is in its realism: none of the men or women Sally and Harry have been with before necessarily represents a negative quality in them that they need to eradicate, they have just matured and outgrown them.

Though there were, then, a few romcoms that took the friends option for their romantic comedy protagonists before *When Harry Met Sally...*, this has become much more popular since the film's success, especially relatively recently. Perhaps this is a commentary on the alienating nature of today's hook-up culture, making choosing a life partner from the ranks of people one has known for a while a particularly comforting prospect; certainly the trope seems to have been steadily increasing in popularity since the start of the twenty-first century.[100]

Romcoms both mainstream and indie now employ the convention; within fourteen months in 2011 and 2012 alone, there were five such films released, all self-consciously playing up the supposed novelty of the best friend as the perfect solution to romantic problems, with the largely interchangeable *Friends with Benefits* and *No Strings Attached*, alongside vehicles for Adam Sandler, *Just Go with It*, and Anna Faris, *What's Your Number?* while in March the next year, indie movie *Friends with Kids* also featured as protagonists friends so close they called each other right after sex – even before their temporary partners left. Of course they ended up together by the end, and they probably had Harry and Sally to thank for that. This film makes the most of being contemporary and alternative, with its bad language and depictions of sex, but the midnight-phone-chats-in-bed trope reveals the lasting debt the genre owes to the older film.

A glance at even more contemporary romcoms shows the friends-to-lovers concept is still prevalent, with 2015's *Sleeping with*

Other People such a clear rerun that it has been dubbed 'When Harry ****ed Sally'[101] and its own director explained it as 'When Harry Met Sally for Assholes'.[102] There seems no end to the intent to revisit the now familiar steps of this fascinating and groundbreaking film.

The ultimate couch couple

Notes

1 'The Vulture Editors', 'Five Great Nora Ephron Movie Scenes', 26 June 2012, http://www.vulture.com/2012/06/five-great-nora-ephron-movie-scenes.html. Accessed 11 June 2015.
2 Bilge Ebiri and David Edelstein, 'The 25 Best Romantic Comedies Since *When Harry Met Sally*', 11 February 2015, http://www.vulture.com/2014/02/25-best-romantic-comedies-since-1989-when-harry-met-sally.html. Accessed 11 June 2015.
3 See Steve Rose, 'Romcoms: The End of the Affair?', *Guardian*, 11 February 2012, http://www.theguardian.com/film/2012/feb/11/rom-coms-end-of-affair. Accessed 11 June 2015. Tatiana Siegel, 'RIP Romantic Comedies: Why Harry Wouldn't Meet Sally in 2013', *The Hollywood Reporter*, 26 September 2013, http://www.hollywoodreporter.com/news/rip-romantic-comedies-why-harry-634776. Accessed 11 June 2015.
4 Helen Gurley Brown, *Sex and the Single Girl* (New York: Bernard Geis Associates, 1962), p. 3.
5 Helen Gurley Brown, *Having It All: Love, Success, Sex, Money, Even if You're Starting with Nothing* (New York: Simon and Schuster, 1982), p. 245.
6 Ibid., p. 206.
7 Ibid., p. 212.
8 Ibid., p. 245.
9 Ibid., p. 214.
10 See, for example, Peter Rainer, 'A Yuppie "Manhattan" Lite: Not Filling', *LA Herald-Examiner*, 14 July 1989, which says the film 'is hip to Manhattan yuppie mores', Academy of Motion Picture Art and Sciences, Margaret Herrick Library, no page, MHL clippings files), and Charles Champlin, 'This Is a Fine Romance', *Los Angeles Times*, 27 July 1989, which contends the film presents 'a recognizable yuppie world, real to the last Reebok', p. 7.
11 Robert Ludlum, *The Icarus Agenda* (New York: Random House, 1988). Herbert Fensterheim, PhD and Jean Baer, *Making Life Right When It Feels All Wrong* (New York: Ransom Associates, 1988).
12 Tom Wolfe, *Mauve Gloves and Madmen, Clutter and Vine* (New York: Farrar, Straus and Giroux, 1976), p. 162.
13 Tamar Jeffers McDonald, *Romantic Comedy: Boy Meets Girl Meets Genre* (London: Wallflower, 2007), p. 61.
14 Nicolaus Mills, 'Culture in an Age of Money', in Nicolaus Mills and Michael Walzer (eds), *50 Years of* Dissent (New Haven, CT: Yale University Press, 2004), p. 173.
15 Ibid.
16 *The Sure Thing* (1985) was a teen romcom, *Stand by Me* (1986) a coming-of-age adventure and *The Princess Bride* (1987) a fairytale romance adventure.
17 Reiner mentions this on both commentaries: Rob Reiner, 'DVD Audio Commentary', *When Harry Met Sally DVD* (2001); Rob Reiner, Billy Crystal and Nora Ephron (2008), 'DVD Audio Commentary'. *When Harry Met Sally... Collector's Edition DVD*. See also Nora Ephron, *The Most of Nora Ephron* (London: Transworld, 2014), p. 211.
18 Andrea King, 'Ephron Wild about "Harry" Nom', *The Hollywood Reporter*, 26 March 1990, p. 9.
19 Ephron, *The Most of Nora Ephron*, p. 211.

20 Jeffers McDonald, *Romantic Comedy*, p. 85.

21 'SH/PKH', Review of *When Harry Met Sally, Screen International*, 17 August 1989, p. 31.

22 King, 'Ephron Wild about "Harry" Nom', p. 9.

23 At this time, though both had appeared in some films, Crystal and Ryan were both best known for television roles, he in comedy *Soap* (ABC) from 1977–81, and she in the actual soap, *As the World Turns*, from 1982–4.

24 Georgia Brown, 'In a Glass Cage', *The Village Voice*, 18 July 1989, p. 68; Elvis Mitchell, 'When Rob Met Woody...' *MLA Weekly*, 21 July 1989, p. 35.

25 Jeffers McDonald, *Romantic Comedy*, p. 76.

26 Julie Salamon, 'Can the Sexes Be Friends without Sex?', *Wall Street Journal*, 13 July 1989 (no page, MHL clippings files).

27 Danny Feingold, '*When Harry Met Sally*... Comedy Wins over Drama', *Village View*, 14–20 July 1989 (no page, MHL clippings files).

28 Mitchell, 'When Rob Met Woody', p. 35.

29 David Ansen, 'To Make True Lovers of Friends', *Newsweek*, 17 July 1989 (no page, MHL clippings files).

30 Richard T. Jameson, 'Meathead's Manhattan', *7 Days*, 19 July 1989 (no page, MHL clippings files).

31 Brown, 'In a Glass Cage', p. 68.

32 See the DVD commentaries, and also Ephron, *The Most of Nora Ephron*, p. 216.

33 Ibid., pp. 215–16.

34 Again, see the DVD commentaries, and also Ephron, *The Most of Nora Ephron*, p. 216.

35 *Daily Variety*, 27 July 1989, p. 9.

36 Sheila Benson, '"Harry Met Sally": A Witty Look at Love', *Los Angeles Times*, 14 July 1989, p. 6.

37 Peter Travers, Review of *When Harry Met Sally...*, *Rolling Stone*, 21 July 1989, http://rollingstone.com/movies/reviews/when-harry-met-sally-19890721. Accessed 11 June 2015.

38 Richard Corliss, 'When Humor Meets Heartbreak', *TIME*, 31 July 1989, p. 65.

39 Champlin, 'This Is a Fine Romance', p. 1.

40 June Pinheiro, 'See Harry & Sally Find Love', *UCLA Summer Bruin*, 13 July 1989 (no page, MHL clippings files).

41 Rita Kempley, 'When Harry Met Sally...', *Washington Post*, 12 July 1989, http://www.washingtonpost.com/wp-srv/style/longterm/movies/videos/enharrymetsallyrkempley_a0c9a5.htm. Accessed 11 June 2015.

42 Duane Byrge, 'When Harry Met Sally...', *The Hollywood Reporter*, 7 July 1989, p. 4.

43 Champlin, 'This Is a Fine Romance', p. 1.

44 Ibid., p. 7.

45 Byrge, 'When Harry Met Sally...', p. 62.

46 Travers, 'Review of *When Harry Met Sally...*'.

47 Byrge, 'When Harry Met Sally...', p. 62.

48 Travers, 'Review of *When Harry Met Sally...*'.

49 Tom Matthews, 'When Harry Met Sally...', *BOXOFFICE*, August 1989 (no page, MHL clippings files).

50 Corliss, 'When Humor Meets Heartbreak', p. 65.

51 See the advertisements in the *Los Angeles Times* on 28 May, p. L1, and 7 July, pp. 16–18.

52 Rainer, 'A Yuppie "Manhattan" Lite'.

53 'SH/PKH', Review of *When Harry Met Sally*, p. 31.

54 Caryn James, 'It's Harry ♥ Sally in a Romance of New Yorkers and Neuroses', *The New York Times*, 12 July 1989 (no page, MHL clippings files).

55 Salamon, 'Can the Sexes Be Friends without Sex?'.

56 'Mac', Weekly *Variety*, 12–18 July 1989, p. 24.

57 Brown, 'In a Glass Cage', p. 68.

58 'SH/PKH', Review of *When Harry Met Sally*, p. 31.

59 Ralph Novak, 'Pics and Pans Review', *People*, 24 July 1989, http://www.people.com/ people/ archive/article/0,,20120800,00.html. Accessed 11 June 2015.

60 Stanley Kauffmann, 'Winding along to Wedlock', *The New Republic*, 21 August 1989, p. 26.

61 Rainer, 'A Yuppie "Manhattan" Lite'.

62 Brown, 'In a Glass Cage', p. 68.

63 Mitchell, 'When Rob Met Woody', p. 35.

64 James, 'It's Harry ♥ Sally in a Romance of New Yorkers and Neuroses'.

65 Feingold, '*When Harry Met Sally...* Comedy Wins over Drama'.

66 Brown, 'In a Glass Cage', p. 68.

67 Jim Emerson, 'Harry Meets Sally, Rob Meets Woody', *The Orange County Register*, 14 July 1989, p. 8.

68 Kauffmann, 'Winding along to Wedlock', p. 26.

69 Emerson, 'Harry Meets Sally, Rob Meets Woody', p. 8.

70 James, 'It's Harry ♥ Sally in a Romance of New Yorkers and Neuroses'.

71 Mitchell, 'When Rob Met Woody', p. 35.

72 Jameson, 'Meathead's Manhattan'.

73 Brown, 'In a Glass Cage', p. 68.

74 Emerson, 'Harry Meets Sally, Rob Meets Woody', p. 8.

75 David Denby, 'At Long Last Friendship', *New York*, 24 July 1989, p. 50.

76 Jay Boyar, 'Woody Allen, Originality – All That's Missing in "Harry"', *Orlando Sentinel*, 21 July 1989, http://articles. orlandosentinel.com/1989-07-21/lifestyle/8907203048_1_woody-allen-harry-met-met-sally. Accessed 11 June 2015.

77 James, 'It's Harry ♥ Sally in a Romance of New Yorkers and Neuroses'.

78 See Brown, 'In a Glass Cage', Emerson, 'Harry Meets Sally, Rob Meets Woody', Feingold, '*When Harry Met Sally...* Comedy Wins over Drama', James, 'It's Harry ♥ Sally in a Romance of New Yorkers and Neuroses', Jameson,'Meathead's Manhattan', 'Mac', Mitchell, 'When Rob Met Woody', Rainer, 'A Yuppie "Manhattan" Lite', Salamon, Can the Sexes Be Friends without Sex?', 'SH/PKH', Review of *When Harry Met Sally*.

79 'Mac', p. 24.

80 James, 'It's Harry ♥ Sally in a Romance of New Yorkers and Neuroses'.

81 See Jeffers McDonald, *Romantic Comedy*, p. 89 and Deborah Jermyn, 'I ♥ NY', in Stacey Abbott and Deborah Jermyn (eds), *Falling in Love Again: Romantic Comedy and Contemporary Cinema* (London: I. B. Tauris, 2009), pp. 9–24.

82 Jeffers McDonald, *Romantic Comedy*.
83 Ephron's montage cuts together over forty comparable moments (singing, dancing, walking, running, kissing) in New York.
84 Emerson, 'Harry Meets Sally, Rob Meets Woody', p. 8.
85 While of course *Oklahoma!* is a stage musical, with successful productions on Broadway before and after the 1955 film, it is perhaps more likely that cinephile Harry would be familiar with the movie version. There is no mention of him having seen the 1979 Broadway revival of the show.
86 Benson, '"Harry Met Sally"', p. 6.
87 Travers, 'Review of *When Harry Met Sally....*'.
88 Martin Shafer, quoted in Martin A. Grove, 'Hollywood Report', *The Hollywood Reporter*, 19 July 1989 (no page, MHL clippings files).
89 Cartoonist Alison Bechdel devised a test in 1985 for contemporary films to see whether or not they were sexist. For a film to pass: '1. It has to have at least two [named] women in it 2. Who talk to each other 3. About something besides a man'. Originally mentioned in *Dykes to Watch Out For*; see the archive at her website, http://dykestowatchoutfor. com/strip-archive-by-number. For the Bechdel test's own web page, see http://bechdeltest.com/. Both accessed 11 June 2015.
90 Nathan Rabin coined this term for a contemporary archetype, the quirky heroine who seems to exist only to teach the neurotic hero how to enjoy life. 'The Bataan Death March of Whimsy Case File #1: *Elizabethtown*', *AV Club*, 25 January 2007, http:// www.avclub.com/article/the-bataan-death-march-of-whimsy-case-file-1-emeli-15577. Accessed 11 June 2015.
91 Gary Sanchez Productions, from 2007, http://www.funnyordie.com/. Accessed 11 June
92 http://www.funnyordie.com/ videos/0247468f28/when-harry-met-sally-2-with-billy-crystal-helen-mirren. Accessed 11 June 2015.
93 See Rose, 'Romcoms', and Siegel, 'RIP Romantic Comedies'.
94 Siegel, 'RIP Romantic Comedies'.
95 Jesse Hassenger, 'Are Rom-coms Just Basically Indie Movies Now or What?', *The L Magazine*, 28 April 2015, http://www.thelmagazine.com/ tag/sleeping-with-other-people/. Accessed 11 June 2015.
96 *The Mindy Project* was cancelled by its originator Fox after three seasons but has since been picked up for a fourth by streaming service Hulu. Other US television romcoms suffered even worse fates: A–Z (NBC, 2014–15) and *Manhattan Love Story* (ABC, 2014), although very overtly borrowing from Ephron, were cancelled after just one season. Alessandra Stanley in 'Rom-com Echoes of Ephron', claims the television series 'find new ways to tell the oldest story: When Harry Friended Sally and You've Got Text', *The New York Times*, 29 September 2014, http://www.nytimes. com/2014/09/30/arts/selfie-a-to-z-and-others-refresh-the-romantic-comedy. html?_r=0. Accessed 11 June 2015. By contrast, (2014) British attempts such as *Scrotal Recall* (Channel 4, 2014) and *Catastrophe* (Channel 4, 2015) have

seemed to fare better, with the former, in particular, revisiting the trope of best friends dating others whilst perfect for each other.

97 Yvonne Roberts, 'What If "Harry Potter Meets Sally" Finally Rekindles Our Passion for the Rom-com?', *Guardian*, 7 August 2014, http://www.theguardian.com/theobserver/she-said/2014/aug/07/what-if-harry-potter-meets-sally-finally-rekindles- our-passion-for-the-rom-com. Accessed 11 June 2014.

98 Kevin O'Keefe, 'Rom-coms Are Back in 2015 – and They're Better Than Ever', Arts.Mic, http://mic.com/articles/116296/rom-coms-are-back-in-2015-and-they-re-better-than-ever. Accessed 11 June 2015.

99 Steve Neale, 'The Big Romance or Something Wild? Romantic Comedy Today', *Screen* vol. 33 no. 3 (1992), pp. 284–99.

100 As with, for example, *Someone Like You* (2001), *Brown Sugar* (2002), *Just Friends* (2005), *Zach And Miri Make a Porno, Sex Drive* and *Made of Honor* (all 2008), *The Switch* and *Valentine's Day* (both 2010), the five 2011–12 films mentioned, *What If* (2013), *Playing It Cool, That Awkward Moment, Love, Rosie* and *Cavemen* (all 2014) and at least *The DUFF* and *Sleeping with Other People* this year, 2015.

101 See Edinburgh Film Festival 2015 website, w.edfilmfest.org.uk/films/2015/sleeping-with-other-people. Accessed 11 June 2015.

102 Justin Morales, Review of *Sleeping with Other People*, Tribeca 2015 report, http://www.iheardthatmoviewas.com/movie-reviews/tribeca-2015-sleeping-with-other-people-review/. Accessed 11 June 2015.

Credits

When Harry Met Sally...
USA/1989

Directed by
Rob Reiner
Produced by
Rob Reiner
Andrew Scheinman
Written by
Nora Ephron
Director of Photography
Barry Sonnenfeld
Production Designer
Jane Musky
Film Editor
Robert Leighton
**Music Adapted and
Arranged by**
Marc Shaiman

©1989. Castle Rock
Entertainment
Production Companies
Castle Rock
Entertainment in
association with Nelson
Entertainment present a
Rob Reiner film
a Columbia Pictures
release

1st Assistant Director
Aaron Barsky
2nd Assistant Director
Michael Waxman
**Additional 2nd
Assistant Directors**
Charles Zalben
Lucille A. OuYang
Forrest L. Futrell

Associate Producer
Nora Ephron
Co-producers
Jeffrey Stott
Steve Nicolaides
Production Manager
Steve Nicolaides
Unit Manager
Mark A. Baker
Location Managers
Donna Bloom
Don Garrison
**Production
Co-ordinators**
Linda Allan
Jane Raab
Hwei-Chu Meng
Production Accountant
Judy Bauer
Assistant Accountants
Donna Santora
Leslie Cornyn
Lynn Goldman
Mr. Reiner's Assistant
Emily Maupin
Production Secretaries
Maura Minsky
Kathy Bond
Nicole Barnum
Shell Hecht
Production Assistants
Lampton Enochs
Joshua Abeles
Edward Fickett
Michael Neumann
Carlyn Bochicchio
Jason Charles
Victoria Cullingham
David Jenkins

Script Supervisor
Kerry Lyn McKissick
Casting by
Jane Jenkins, c.s.a.
Janet Hirshenson, c.s.a.
Casting Associates
Michael Hirshenson
Robin Allan
Camera Operator
M. Todd Henry
Assistant Camera
Angelo DiGiacomo
Brian Armstrong
Christopher Duskin
Thomas Miligan
Gaffers
Russell W. Engels
Kevin Kelley
Key Grip
Dennis Gamiello
Video by
Video Image
Greg McMurray
[McMurry]
Still Photographers
Andy Schwartz
Bruce Birmelin
Assistant Editors
Steve Nevius
Debbie Goldsmith
Norman Buckley
Negative Cutting
Gary Burritt
**Art Department
Co-ordinator**
Harold Thrasher
Set Decorators
George R. Nelson
Sabrina Wright-Basile
Scenic Artist
Billy Puzo

Prop Masters
David L. Glazer
Dick Tice
Props
James J. Archer
**Construction
Co-ordinator**
Frank Viviano
Costumes Designed by
Gloria Gresham
Costume Supervisor
Jennifer L. Parsons
Meg Ryan's Make-up
Stephen Abrums
Joseph A. Campayno
Billy Crystal's Make-up
Kenneth Chase
Peter Montagna
Hairstylists
Barbara Lorenz
William A. Farley
Titles & Opticals
Pacific Title
**Special Musical
Performances and
Arrangements by**
Harry Connick, Jr.
Harry Connick, Jr. Trio
Harry Connick, Jr.
Ben Wolfe
Ralph Penland
Music Supervisor
Scott Stambler
Orchestrations by
Marc Shaiman
Thom Sharp
Music Scoring Mixer
John Richards
Music Recording by
Evergreen Recording

Re-recorded by
Buena Vista Sound
Studios
Soundtrack
'It Had to Be You' written
by Isham Jones, Gus
Kahn, [1] performed by
Frank Sinatra, [2]
performed by Harry
Connick, Jr. Trio; 'Our
Love Is Here to Stay'
written by George
Gershwin, Ira Gershwin,
[1] performed by Louis
Armstrong, Ella
Fitzgerald, [2] performed
by Harry Connick, Jr.;
'Don't Pull Your Love'
written by Brian Potter,
Dennis Lambert,
performed by Hamilton,
Joe Frank & Reynolds;
'Ramblin' Man' written
by Forrest Richard
[Dickey] Betts, performed
by Allman Brothers; 'Its
the Right Time of the
Night (for Making Love)'
written by Peter McCan
[McCann], performed by
Jennifer Warnes; 'Let's
Call the Whole Thing Off'
written by George
Gershwin, Ira Gershwin,
[1] performed by Louis
Armstrong, Ella
Fitzgerald, [2] performed
by Harry Connick, Jr. Trio;
'Where or When' written
by Lorenz Hart, Richard
Rodgers, performed by

Ella Fitzgerald; 'Lady's
Lunch' written by Marc
Shaiman; 'The Tables
Have Turned' written by
Laura Kenyon, Marc
Shaiman, Scott Wittman;
'But Not for Me' written
by George Gershwin, Ira
Gershwin, performed by
Harry Connick, Jr.; 'Plane
Cue' and 'La Marseillaise'
(from 'Casablanca')
written by Max Steiner;
'Autumn in New York'
written by Vernon Duke,
performed by Harry
Connick, Jr. Trio; 'Winter
Wonderland' written by
Felix Bernard, Dick
Smith, performed by Ray
Charles; 'I Could Write a
Book' written by Lorenz
Hart, Richard Rodgers,
vocal by Harry Connick,
Jr.; 'The Surrey with the
Fringe on Top' written by
Richard Rodgers, Oscar
Hammerstein II; 'Say It
Isn't So' written by Irving
Berlin; 'Stompin' at the
Savoy' written by Benny
Goodman, Chick Webb,
Edgar Sampson, Andy
Razaf, performed by
Harry Connick, Jr. Trio;
'Mozart String Quintet – E
Flat Major' written by
Wolfgang Amadeus
Mozart; 'Don't Be That
Way' written by Edgar
Sampson, Benny

Goodman, Mitchell Parish; 'Have Yourself a Merry Little Christmas' written by Ralph Blane, Hugh Martin, performed by Bing Crosby; 'Call Me' written by Tony Hatch; 'Don't Get around Much Anymore' written by Duke Ellington, Bob Russell, vocal by Harry Connick, Jr.; 'Isn't It Romantic?' written by Lorenz Hart, Richard Rodgers

Sound Mixer
Robert Eber
Boom Operators
John K. Fundus
George Baetz
Re-recording Mixers
Terry Porter, C.A.S.
Mel Metcalfe
David J. Hudson
Supervising Sound Editors
Charles L. Campbell
Louis L. Edemann
Sound Editors
Richard C. Franklin, Jr.
Larry Carow
Chuck Meely [Neely]
Paul Timothy Carden
Assistant Sound Editor
Pam Kimber
Supervising ADR Editor
Larry Singer
Assistant ADR Editor
Rod Rogers
Dubbing Recordist
David Gertz

Foley Mixer
Dean Drabin
Transportation Co-ordinators
Tim Roslan
James E. Fanning
Publicists
Nancy Seltzer & Associates, Inc.
Wilkinson/Lipsman
Legal Services provided by
O'Melveny & Myers
Cranes and Dollys by
Chapman
Lighting and Grip Equipment supplied by
Lee Lighting America, Ltd.
Photographic Equipment by
Panavision
Film Excerpts
clip from 'Casablanca' [1942] provided by Turner Entertainment Co.
'Dick Clark New Year's Rockin' Eve' [1983] courtesy of Dick Clark Media Archives
Air Transportation and Landing Footage provided by
United Airlines
Producers wish to thank
Tina Nielsen and Jay Cooper; The University of Chicago; The Buffalo Bill Football Organization; NFL Films, CD Banzai! (Los Angeles); Ronnie Davis

and The Washington Street Cafe Caterers; and the New York City Mayor's Office of Film, Theatre & Broadcasting for their support in making this film

A special thanks to Sol Horn for his inspiration
Original Motion Picture Soundtrack Album available on
Columbia Records, Cassettes and Compact Discs

CAST
Billy Crystal
Harry Burns
Meg Ryan
Sally Albright
Carrie Fisher
Marie
Bruno Kirby
Jess
Steven Ford
Joe
Lisa Jane Persky
Alice
Michelle Nicastro
Amanda Reese
Gretchen Palmer
stewardess
Robert Alan Beuth
man on aisle
David Burdick
9 year old boy
Joe Viviani
judge
Harley [Jane] Kozak
Helen Hillson

Joseph Hunt
waiter at wedding
Kevin Rooney
Ira Stone
Franc Luz
Julian
Tracy Reiner
Emily
Kyle Heffner
Gary
Kimberley LaMarque
waitress
Stacey Katzin
hostess
Estelle Reiner
older woman customer
John Arceri
Christmas tree salesman
Peter Day
joke teller at wedding
Kuno Sponholz
Connie Sawyer
Charles Dugan
Katherine Squire
Al Christy
Frances Chaney
Bernie Hern
Rose Wright
Aldo Rossi
Donna Hardy
Peter Pan

Jane Chung
documentary couples
uncredited
Rob Reiner
New Year's Eve
countdown voice
Nicholas Glaeser
waiter
Production Details
Filmed from 29 August
1988 to 15 November
1988 on location in East
Village and Greenwich
Village (Manhattan, New
York City, New York),
Coney Island (Brooklyn,
New York City, New York),
East Rutherford (New
Jersey), Lake Shore Drive
and Hyde Park (Chicago,
Illinois) and Wilmington
(Los Angeles, California)
and at Silvercup Studios
(New York City, New York)
and Hollywood Center
Studios (Hollywood,
California, USA). Budget:
$16,000,000
35mm; 1.85:1; in colour:
colour by DuArt Film
Laboratories (New York

City) and CFI (Hollywood,
California), prints by
DeLuxe; sound - Dolby
stereo; MPAA: 29800
Shooting Title
Harry, This Is Sally
Pre-shooting Title
Boy Meets Girl
Script Title
How They Met

Release Details
US theatrical release
(limited) by Columbia
Pictures on 12 July 1989;
in general release from 21
July 1989. MPAA rating: R.
running time: 96 minutes
UK theatrical release by
Palace Pictures on 1
December 1989. BBFC
certificate:
15 (no cuts). running
time: 95 minutes 28
seconds / 8,591 feet +15
frames

Credits compiled by
Julian Grainger

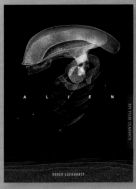